T0244895

A N G E L S

D E M O N S

JOHN R. GILHOOLY

ANGELS

DEMONS

WHAT THE BIBLE SAYS ABOUT
SPIRITUAL CREATURES

PUBLISHING®
BRENTWOOD, TENNESSEE

Printed by B&H Publishing Group
Brentwood, Tennessee

Dewey Decimal Classification: 235
Subject Heading: ANGELS / DEVIL / SPIRITS

Unless otherwise noted, all Scripture references are taken from the Christian Standard Bible. Copyright © 2017 by Holman Bible Publishers. Used by permission. Christian Standard Bible®, and CSB® are federally registered trademarks of Holman Bible Publishers, all rights reserved.

Cover design by Faceout Studio, Molly von Borstel. Upper image: *The Hunting of the Snark* from Paradise Lost. Artwork by Gustave Doré, from DL5MDA/wikimedia commons, Public Domain. Lower image: *The Woman and Dragon* by Gustave Doré from Nicku/shutterstock. Texture by detchana wangkheeree/shutterstock. Ampersand by Blue Flourishes/shutterstock. Author photo by Scott Huck.

1 2 3 4 5 6 • 27 26 25 24

DEDICATION

mo labrad
rop tú molas cen mannrad
rop tú charas mo chride
a Rí nime ocus talman.

This anonymous Irish poem, originating between the
twelfth and fifteenth centuries, says,
My speech—
may it praise you perfectly,
may my heart love you,
King of heaven and earth.

Selecting this poem is a nod to my Irish heritage and
also captures the spirit in which I offer this book: that it
helps us to praise and love our King more deeply.

ACKNOWLEDGMENTS

Writing a book is a challenge. Authors attempt to imagine what readers will hear and what they will understand, where they might misunderstand or object, where to contest, where to encourage, or where to make a joke. You can never say all the things you hoped to say, but you still have to do all the typing. At the end of all that, you are not even sure whether anyone will read the thing. So my first acknowledgment is to you, as a reader: thank you for picking up this book and considering what I have written.

Writing acknowledgments is similarly difficult. Nevertheless, God demands we show honor where it is due. I would like to thank my colleagues for their encouragement, their advice, and their correction as I wrote this book. I do not want to single any of them out because Ched Spellman is easily embarrassed. I'll also mention Brandon Smith, Michael Shepherd, Trent Rogers, and Ronni Kurtz.

I would like to thank Matthew Hawkins and the team at B&H Publishing Group for overseeing the process of taking some stuff I wrote down and turning it into a book. Their time, insight, and effort have been a blessing to me.

I am a private person and so rarely publish information about my family. But my wife tells me that if authors do not thank their families, then apparently readers may think of them as monsters. Since I am not a monster, I would very much like to thank my wife and children.

I am also supposed to take responsibility for all the things I said that aren't correct, so presto! I have thus taken responsibility.

Soli Deo Gloria.

CONTENTS

CONTENTS

CHAPTER 1

WHAT ARE ANGELS, AND
WHAT DO THEY DO?

I returned to my office from teaching one afternoon
to see the little red light on my desk phone blinking.
I picked up the phone and clicked through all the
menus to access my voicemail.

"You have one unheard message."

Yup, I thought, *I saw the blinky light.*

The message was unusual. Well, I should say, you probably would have thought it was unusual. The speaker—let's
call him Greg—was calling the university to see if anyone
there knew anything about angels. He said he had called
the main university phone line and been directed to my
phone number. He had taken a home video of an angel—in

fact, he said, it was Michael the archangel—and it was important that he speak with me about what he had seen.

Why did I get the call? Because I'm an angelologist. Yes, that is a real job. Biologists study living things, and geologists study rocks. I study angels.

What's more, I guess you could say I'm a reluctant angelologist. The reason? I just don't think angels are that important. Interesting? Absolutely. Source of endless speculation? You bet. Central to our faith? No. However, from how popular the angels are in culture, fiction, and Christian books, you would be forgiven if you thought they were smack in the center of the Christian religion. That's why I'm reluctant. I spend most of my time responding to questions about angelology saying, "Well, no. Not really."

You know what can be a real killjoy? Always having to be the killjoy.

Back to Greg. I asked him a series of questions when we finally met on the phone. Did he know God made the world? Did he know about sin? Did he know that the only way to be saved is to repent and believe in the Lord Jesus? My main goal in returning phone calls like Greg's is to see if the person calling has heard the message of Jesus Christ. Greg said he knew all those things. He was a believer. If that is the case, I don't care as much if they have some odd views on angels. I'd like to straighten those out, of course. But we need to keep the main thing the main thing.

I heard you have some questions about angels.

Yes! In fact, I have a video of Michael the archangel in my living room.

Let me ask you something, Greg. How do you know that the angel was Michael? Did he talk to you?

No. But he had a symbol, and when I searched for it on the Internet, I found that it was listed in a book seven hundred years older than the Scriptures.

Let me pause and say there is no such book. I imagine he read something about the Book of Enoch, a non-Christian composite book from the first century. It is not older than most of the Scripture, and it reflects a different religion than Christianity.

I'm not sure about that, Greg. Would you be willing to share the video with me?

The image Greg had captured in the video was smoke, from a candle perhaps. I told him I was not going to be able to confirm his video for him. We talked for a while about why.

As I said, I get these kinds of calls or emails fairly frequently. None of the videos have ever been of an angel, and I don't expect that one of them will be. Sometimes this viewpoint strikes people as odd. After all, aren't angels real? Why be skeptical?

Let me respond. Of course, they are real. Angels are some of the things God made when he created everything.

They are as real as squirrels, rocks, and rutabagas. They are real, moral, rational agents just like us, except they don't have bodies. They are spiritual, celestial creatures. They are "ministering spirits sent out to serve those who are going to inherit salvation" (Heb. 1:14). So, why the skepticism on my part?

Because there is lots of unhealthy or downright misleading speculation about angels. The Bible doesn't just tell us what the angels are; it also tells us what they do. Here's the kicker: the Holy Scriptures do not say much about angels. They are depicted doing only a handful of things, and they stay largely behind the scenes. The occasional glimpse behind the curtain is not an invitation to go backstage.

The Scriptures are more concerned with Jesus than they are with angels. That should be important to us. What the Bible cares about is what we should care about. More to the point, the central concerns of the Scripture should orient our central concerns. After all, the worldview of the biblical authors is a Christian worldview because the Bible is a Christian book. This understanding not only sets the trajectory for how we should read the Bible but also for what should get the most attention in our theology and in our walk with Christ. The more I have studied angels in history and in the Scriptures, the more convinced I have become that we need to say less about angels: we just need to say less more clearly.

The Word *Angel* in Scripture

In fact, the biblical languages (Hebrew, Aramaic, and Greek) do not have a unique word for "angel." In those languages, the word we most typically translate into English as "angel" is the word meaning "messenger." Sometimes this word refers to a human messenger, as in "Jezebel sent a messenger to Elijah" (1 Kings 19:2). In other cases, the word refers to a heavenly or celestial messenger, what we call an angel (Luke 3:13–14). The literary context is what helps translators decide which English word is appropriate.

In this book, it will sometimes be helpful to refer to the word for angel in the biblical languages; but I promise you won't need any previous knowledge about biblical languages, translation, or linguistics. We should begin, however, by deciding how we will refer to the biblical words for angel.

I will do this using what linguists call transliteration. Transliteration is the process by which we take the sounds of a word in one language and write letters that represent those sounds in another language. This is a tricky process because some languages—like English—have surprising customs for spelling and pronunciation. Furthermore, not all languages have the same sounds. Nevertheless, transliteration is helpful because it allows a reader to make sense of how to say a word in a language they cannot read or speak.

In our text, the Hebrew and Aramaic word for angel will be represented as *malak*. The Greek word for angel will be represented as *angelos*. Using these words, *malak* and *angelos*, will help us see when the translation is doing some of the interpretive work for us in understanding our Bibles. It is okay when this happens, but—as we grow in our understanding of the Scriptures—we want to be increasingly aware of when it does.

Of course, some other words also refer to angels in Scripture. These words, like the words *malak* and *angelos*, sometimes refer to angels and sometimes do not. For example, the basic word *spirit* (Greek: *pneuma*) sometimes refers to an angelic figure (Heb. 1:14). In some cases, "sons of God" (Hebrew: *bene elohim*) does as well (Job 1:6). Angels are also called the host or army (*tsabaoth*) of heaven (Ps. 148:2). There are also words for specific kinds of spiritual beings, such as the Hebrew words *seraphim* (Isa. 6:2) or *cherubim* (Ezek. 10:1), although these are rarely used. The main words are *malak* and *angelos*.

Notice something interesting about these words. Because they mean "messenger," they already tell us something about what the angels normally are and what they normally do. Most often in the Bible, we find angels delivering an important message or assisting someone in delivering or understanding a message.

In fact, the appearances of angels in the Bible can be described in five ways, or motifs:

1. Angels worship the living God (as all creatures should).
2. Angels protect or guide a key figure(s) in a Bible story.
3. Angels announce or execute God's judgment.
4. Angels announce a significant birth.
5. Angels deliver a message to someone or interpret a message to a prophet.

We see examples of each of these activities in the Book of Moses: Genesis through Deuteronomy. The rest of the Old and New Testaments give repeated examples of these activities. However, the pattern established in the first five books of the Bible continues through the rest of Holy Scripture.

A Word about Method

Why is it important to see this pattern? Because our talk about angels should follow the pattern of the Bible's talk about angels. In other words, our theology should speak the same language as the Scriptures. I want to persuade you that we need to keep our view of the angels in proportion to what the biblical authors say about them. To do that, we must remember two important things.

First, the Bible doesn't mention angels that often. The words *malak* and *angelos* appear only a few hundred times. Recall that those words do not always mean "angel." In fact, I have listed all the times they do mean "angel" in the back of this book. It is a pretty short list of verses.

Second, even when angels appear, the Bible does not discuss them; rather it mentions them. We will see some examples of this discussion/mention distinction in subsequent chapters. For now, what this means for us is that the Bible does not say much about angels. If the Bible doesn't say much about angels, then maybe we should not try to say too much either.

Nevertheless, we do want to speak clearly about what the Bible says, so we must spend some time reflecting on what the biblical authors say about angels. In each of the next several chapters, I will discuss the important passages for angelology in a section of Holy Scripture. Mining the Scriptures to discuss a particular topic is challenging and requires some care, especially when the topic is not one the biblical authors discuss explicitly. After all, when we read the Bible, our main goal should be to listen to what the biblical authors want to tell us. The reason this should be our goal is because the Bible is the written Word of God, and the human authors of Scripture (Moses, David, Matthew, and so on) are inspired by God to tell the story they are going to tell, each in his own way (2 Tim. 3:16; 2 Pet. 1:20–21). If Moses is inspired of God to tell us a particular story, we can be confident he knows better than we do what we need to see and hear. This fact remains true even when he does not tell us some things we would like to know. God has not promised us answers to all our questions of curiosity (Deut. 29:29). So our first posture as Bible readers must be one of listening. Reading is first and foremost about listening to what the black print on white paper says.

Now, as we faithfully read the Bible, we discover that certain words or ideas crop up over and over again. Pretty soon, some of these concepts almost leap off the page at us. This phenomenon happens because all the biblical writers are God's writers telling us the story God wants us to know. He doesn't hide what he wants his people to know behind fancy words, maps, and historical events we don't remember. Nor are his prophets simply improving the myths of other ancient peoples. No, instead, God has his prophets put down in human language what we ought to think about him and his plans, as well as how we should interpret miracles, history, and human experience. So the repeated ideas and words we see in Scripture can serve us as clues as to what is most important. In fact, the pressure we feel in seeing some words and ideas again and again should cause us to make claims about what the world is really like.

When we come to the Bible with theological questions—like: What is an angel? What do they do?—we should start by trying to discern those places where the text pushes us to make certain claims because of the steady repetition of the biblical authors' instruction. Of course, if we start by trying only to answer our own questions, we will end up treating the Bible like an encyclopedia with entries on all our pet questions and interests. This treatment is dangerous because it may convince us that we can skip the first step of theology, which is listening to the Word of God.

Hence, our goal in this book will be second-step theology. We are trying to reflect on what the repetition of Scripture causes us to say about angels. Doing this well assumes we have already been listening carefully to the biblical authors. Part of this careful listening means we are not going to put words into the mouths of the biblical authors. Unfortunately, lots of teaching on angels in contemporary Christian life does just that. Lots of teaching on angels begins with exposition about the background assumptions of the biblical authors, assumptions that forget the prophets are not merely men of their own time. They are God's prophets.

Because the writers of Holy Scripture are inspired of God, we need to be careful that our curiosity does not cause us to enlarge what the biblical authors say. Hence, I will try to distinguish clearly between what we can read in Scripture and what I think we can reasonably infer from the repetition and pressure of the whole Bible. Attempting to distinguish between those two things can be difficult, but it is an important practice for Christians.

In what follows, I am going to walk through sections of Scripture and identify examples of the key motifs. Not every book of Scripture mentions angels, and not every mention is equally significant for our purposes: hence, we will focus on major sections of Scripture and not every individual book of the Bible. As we do, we will begin to understand what the Bible says about the heavenly host.

CHAPTER 2

THE BOOK OF MOSES

I probably get less email than you do because my students know I don't like email. But when you have a contact form on your university website, you get random emails about all kinds of things. Books someone wants you to purchase, for example. Diatribes about "new" interpretations of (usually) Revelation. Accounts of visions. I get quite a few random emails about angels, demons, spiritual experiences, and paranormal stuff. I get a lot of phone calls from pastors also, usually because one of their church members read some newfangled book and becomes suddenly odd or argumentative about spirits or what the Bible really says about the host of heaven. Paul says, "Knowledge puffs up" (1 Cor. 8:1). He is surely right. But sometimes ignorance puffs up too.

If angels and demons do not come up much in your pastor's preaching, that is a good thing. That probably just means he is serious about listening to the Word of God first. And the Bible doesn't talk about the spiritual realm all that much.

Yet something about the spiritual realm entices people, doesn't it? All this kind of spooky mystical stuff makes for good theater. There's a reason people like supernatural shows and movies, even scary ones. There is a reason there are four hundred books on angels and magic and channeling and crystals at your local used bookshop. People are drawn to spiritual things. When someone can offer a confident system for explaining all this stuff without hesitation or a simple "I don't know," they can offer something really attractive to the general public. If that system is based on obscure books from an ancient place, so much the better.

Here is the problem for Christians: when people want to come up with extra information about this stuff, they cannot go to the Bible. Why? Because the prophets don't talk that much about it. The biblical authors acknowledge there are angels (and demons), and then they move on. They keep them behind the scenes for a reason. So books on angels and demons have to rely on questionable information from other sources, like other ancient religions or religious books or anecdotes from exotic lands. Most of that stuff is simply nonsense. But, even if some of it turns out to be right (and how would we know?), it is beside the point for Christians. If we want to know what the Bible teaches about angels (or demons), then our object of study should be the Bible. We can trust that what it tells us is sufficient for us. God's Word tells us what we need to know.

Because I believe that wholeheartedly, I plan to walk through the Bible and talk about all the times the word *angel* crops up. One of the things I hope this shows you is that—in the grand story of the Bible—angels are not a big deal. (Remember, I am a reluctant angelologist.)

In this chapter, we start with the Book of Moses. The Book of Moses contains the biblical books of Genesis, Exodus, Leviticus, Numbers, and Deuteronomy. Not all these books mention angels, but the pattern we see in these books sets up our expectations for what angels are like and what they do in the rest of the Bible. The motifs I mentioned in the previous chapter will all make a first showing in this first section of Holy Scripture. Even though angels are relatively minor background characters in these books, their appearances tell us a lot about how we should understand them and their function.

Genesis

Let's start at the beginning with the week of God's creation. You would expect, perhaps, that Moses would tell us something about the creation of angels in Genesis 1. After all, the book says God created the heavens and the earth, which is a Hebrew way of saying that God made all the stuff. Yet Moses's focus is on physical creation—the world in much the way we now know it, as well as the land in which he will put Adam and Eve. He talks about all the physical sorts of creatures and features—such as water, sky, and land—that are important for us and our sustenance. He even talks about the sun, moon, and stars, which we need to keep the calendar of festivals and work the land. But he doesn't say anything about the creation of the angels in the first two chapters of his book. Angels do not make an appearance until the end of chapter 3, where they serve as a message that there is something sacred and powerful in the garden, something that has been lost.

There may be a lesson in this for us. As long as there have been Christians, there have been questions about why Moses does not describe the creation of the angels in Genesis 1. Sometimes these questions of curiosity have been indulged with speculative answers or by examining what different ancient religions or philosophies say about creatures, gods, and heavenly beings. That is not the wisest approach for Christians.

Instead, we should reframe our questions in light of what the authors of Scripture have already chosen to write down. My favorite example of this method comes from an eighth-century clergyman named Alcuin (Al-Kwin). He wrote a commentary on the book of Genesis that consisted of common questions he had received about Genesis along with his answers. One of the early questions is about why Moses does not describe the creation of the angels or the subsequent fall of the devil. Alcuin responds by saying that Moses does not describe such things because God had not planned salvation for the angels. In other words, Genesis isn't about angels or demons; it is about God's plan for his people. The things Moses chose to write down are things that contribute to the story he is inspired of God to tell. That story may not answer all our questions of curiosity, but it is the story we need to hear.

As I mentioned, the first appearance of the host of heaven in the book is in chapter 3, where God sets a cherub to guard the entrance to the garden of Eden. I'll have more to say about cherubim in a later chapter, but for now notice that the presence of the angel outside the garden sends a clear message. In fact, as the characters of Genesis approach the boundaries of the land God had promised to his people, we often find an angelic encounter. This becomes a method to highlight the importance of God's promises.

The first appearance of an angel as a character in Scripture comes in Genesis 16, when the angel meets Hagar on the road. Hagar had recently conceived a child with Abram, but Hagar had fled from his camp because Sarah, Abram's wife, had dealt with her harshly. Sarah acted this way even though it was her idea for Abram to conceive a child with Hagar. The angel commands her to return to Sarah and tells her that she will be blessed with many children. He also instructs her what name she should give to her firstborn.

Some interpreters believe this angel is God because the angel speaks at first with a first-person pronoun ("I will greatly multiply" in verse 10). This is a common but mistaken interpretation, for notice that when God hears the voice of Hagar's child in Genesis 21, we read: "God heard the boy crying, and the angel of God called to Hagar from heaven and said to her, 'What's wrong, Hagar? Don't be afraid, for God has heard the boy crying from the place where he is'" (v. 17). Moses clearly distinguishes between the Lord and the angel of the Lord. It is true that angels are often representatives of God in much the same way his prophets are, but they are not God. For now, notice that the motif of birth announcement is marked in this episode (motif 4). The angel not only confirms that Hagar will bear a child but also that God has specific plans for the child and for his family.

Angels also arrive on the scene in Genesis 18 and 19, surrounding the story of Abraham and Lot. However, they are presented with a great deal of ambiguity. In other words, their description might leave us with many questions. To begin, the figures are not initially called angels but rather "men," *anakim*. In fact, in the whole of chapter 18, the word *angel* does not appear. Only in the first verse of chapter 19 do we find that these men are *malakim* ("im" makes the word plural here). Should we take this word to mean messengers or angels? Traditionally, these figures are understood to be angels, and I think that is the right interpretation. Reflecting on this example is a good way to see how a translator could decide how to understand an ambiguous word like *malak*.

After all, there are good reasons in the text to believe the figures are not merely human messengers. First, these figures appear and disappear with no significant warning or introduction. Second, they are able to overpower "the men of the city" (Gen. 19:4) in rescuing Lot (19:10). Third, they strike the men of the city with blindness (19:5). Considering these details in the story, it is difficult to see these *malakim* as merely human messengers. Furthermore, the angels fit the pattern: they protect a key figure in the story as well as execute judgment (motifs 2 and 3).

These two instances (Gen. 16 and Gen. 18–19) are somewhat conspicuous because the angels not only appear in both, but they appear as central characters of those stories. Even so, the angels are still mentioned in an oblique way. We do not receive specific details about them. There is little discussion of them. However, they remain central, speaking characters. That itself is unusual. More often, we find angels are peripheral or background characters. This is because of the central motif of the angels, which is that they bring a significant message to a significant character. Often (but not always) the message is more important than the messenger.

In the same way angels spoke with people in earlier chapters, an angel calls Abraham to stop him from sacrificing his son Isaac in Genesis 22:11. Through the angel's message in Genesis 22:16–18, God then confirms the promise that he had made to Abraham in Genesis 15 (motif 5).

In Genesis 24, Abraham tells his servant that God will send an angel before him as he seeks a wife for his son. In the chapter, no further mention is made of the angel— nothing is said about what he looks like, how he leads the servant, or what he does. Yet the servant is clear that the Lord had prospered his journey by leading him to the correct house (Gen. 24:27). In that verse, he does not speak about an angel, as if the phrase "his angel before you" (v. 7) had been merely a blessing or a kind of well-wish. He speaks as though there really was another creature with him, one of God's servants to protect him on the journey (motif 2).

Nevertheless, the servant makes clear in his explanation of his journey that Abraham had told him God would send an angel with him to ensure success on the journey (Gen. 24:40). The angel was how God led the servant on the "right way" (Gen. 24:48). Even though the servant is confident the angel went before him, the angel never appears as a character in the story. He remains in the background. We do not learn the servant's name, but we do hear him speak. We never even see the angel. The message is the main thing.

By contrast, in Genesis 28, there is a famous scene in which Jacob dreams of angels ascending and descending on a "stairway" (v. 12). The text does not specify what the angels are doing, but they are somehow participants in the vision God gives to Jacob at Bethel. The angels were there to look in on what God was doing with Jacob, as Peter says they long to do (1 Pet. 1:21), and hence to bear witness to the truth of God's promises. This is the proper job of a messenger and a worshipper of the living God. They are not the focal point of the scene; rather, the angels are there as a witness to what God is doing. Perhaps that is why Jesus tells Nathaniel that he also will see "heaven opened and the angels of God ascending and descending on the Son of Man" (John 1:51). The angels are peripheral, yet they adorn the witness of God and communicate his messages when directed. For Jacob, the angels are early signs to him (messages) that he is encountering a message from the God of his fathers. Think of them like theme music. They let you know the show is starting. When there are angels, something exciting happens. They are not casual acquaintances.

For example, in Genesis 31, Jacob recounts that an angel had shared with him God's message in a dream that Jacob should return to his home, saying, "I am the God of Bethel, where you poured oil on the stone marker and made a solemn vow to me. Get up, leave this land, and return to your native land" (Gen. 31:13). Jacob is reminded by an angel of what God intends for him—in fact, the presence of the angel in the dream is part of the reminder that this message is from God, the God Jacob swore to at Bethel where the angels ascended and descended before him. He is thus able to associate the presence of the angels with the presence of God.

Hence, as God guides Jacob back to the land, he encounters the angels again (Gen. 32). They become a sign for him that God would have him camp in that place. This encampment sets up the wrestling encounter at Peniel, in which Jacob wrestles with an angel during the night. In his prevailing with the angel, Jacob is blessed (Gen. 32:28). Jacob sees this wrestling as having "seen God face to face" (v. 30), although he does not in fact see God. This incident highlights for us again the ambiguity of the angels in Scripture. Like Samson's parents in Judges 13, there is confusion on the part of the characters between the angel (Judg. 13:21) and God himself (Judg. 13:22). Hosea makes clear that Jacob struggled with an angel by clarifying a potentially ambiguous word with the clearer one: "As a man he struggled with *elohim* [usually God, but sometimes angel, foreign gods, or human judges]. He struggled with *malak* and overcame him" (Hosea 12:3–4). This is the same clarification found in Genesis 48, when years later Jacob blesses his son Joseph: "The God before whom my fathers Abraham and Isaac walked, the God who has been my shepherd all my life to this day, the angel who has redeemed me from all harm—may he bless these boys" (Gen. 48:15–16). As Moses tells us the story, he shows us the development in Jacob's understanding of the Lord.

The difference between Jacob's explanation of his experience in Genesis 32 and Genesis 48 has to do with the events of chapters 34 and 35. In those chapters, as Jacob comes to form a personal commitment to the Lord ("the God of Israel," Gen. 33:20), God reiterates the blessing to Jacob (Gen. 25:11–13). This message comes to him at Bethel, and there is no longer any mention of the angels. This transition is an example of the dynamism of Jacob's character. For example, consider the dream Jacob has at the end of his life when he is going to see his son Joseph in Egypt. At that time, God calls to him in a vision and speaks with him directly. No longer does Jacob's encounter with God include the presence and sign of angels. Moses shows how Jacob has grown in his understanding and his relationship to the Lord. As Bible readers, we want to grow in the same way.

Hence, we must allow the narrator of the text to tell us how to understand what the angels are and what they are doing. This caution is best expressed by patience and by carefully distinguishing between what a character says and what the inspired author of the book wants to say to us. Even when an author of Scripture tells part of his own story, as for example Moses will do, there is still a difference between what the character knew at the time and what the author knows at the time he composes his book under the inspiration of the Holy Spirit of God.

Considering our reflection on the role of angels in Genesis, we can note something interesting about the Joseph story that concludes the book: the angels make no significant appearance in those chapters of the book at all. Joseph is not in the land that had been promised because of his capture and slavery in Egypt. Yet God is with him (Gen. 39:21) so that he meets with success in trials, flees temptation, interprets dreams, and has great understanding. Even the pagan king confesses that Joseph has the spirit of God in him (41:37), after Joseph tells Pharoah that God will enable Joseph to interpret his dreams. Joseph knows that his success is from God (45:9) and that all his paths were guided by a God who keeps his promises (45:5–7). His understanding is purer than Jacob's had been.

In Genesis the angels have delivered messages in dreams and visions, have guided and protected key figures in God's stories, and highlighted the presence of God through their worship of him. It will not be until Moses encounters the angel in the burning bush that they make another appearance to announce the presence of God.

Exodus

The scene of the burning bush is one of the more famous stories in Holy Scripture. In the Bible, Moses encounters an angel in the midst of a flaming bush that is on fire but somehow not consumed by the flames. This angel brings Moses God's message, which instructs him to go to Egypt to deliver the people from their slavery there. The angel's presence in the burning bush is the means God uses to arouse his attention. The text does not say that Moses saw the angel but rather that he noticed the bush that was not consumed by the flames (Exod. 3:3). After Moses walks over to see the bush, the Lord calls out to him from the bush (3:4). The mention of the angel is cursory here.

What is important is that the presence of the angel and fire signals that the voice Moses hears and the person to whom he speaks is God—"the God of your father, the God of Abraham, the God of Isaac, and the God of Jacob" (motif 5; Exod. 3:6). To repeat an illustration: the angels serve in this way like divine theme music. They let you know the real show is about to start. Moses is surprised by this encounter because at this time he does not really know who or even what God is.

Hence, Moses attempts to hide his face from God (Exod. 3:6), and he asks the Lord who he is and what his name is (3:11, 13). We know from later in the book that Moses, the author, has learned more than he knew at the time he spoke to God at the burning bush, for in Exodus 33 Moses asks God to show him God's glory. God tells him at that time that no one may see him and live (33:20). But back in Exodus 3, Moses does not know such things.

Some interpreters believe the angel is God, but that is not consistent with the passage or the interpretation of the passage in the New Testament. In Acts 7:30–32, Stephen says: "After forty years had passed, an angel appeared to him in the wilderness of Mount Sinai, in the flame of a burning bush. When Moses saw it, he was amazed at the sight. As he was approaching to look at it, the voice of the Lord came: I am the God of your ancestors—the God of

Abraham, of Isaac, and of Jacob. Moses began to tremble and did not dare to look" (see Exod. 30–32).

We have to let Scripture interpret Scripture for us. Stephen helps us understand that what Moses encountered was the angel, a presence that announced that the voice he heard was God's voice. God had not yet come in the flesh to be among his people (John 1:14). Instead, his presence was mediated by his messengers, both angelic and human.

In fact, the angels continue to appear in Exodus in behind-the-scenes ways. For example, an angel goes before the people to protect and guide them (Exod. 14:19). Recall that this is the same language as the behind-the-scenes angel in Genesis 24. Again, this language is repeated in Exodus 23, 32, and 33. The angel is sent by God to go before the people, to guide them and make their way clear (motif 2). Sending an angel before them was the way God chose to lead the people (Exod. 13:21–22; 14:19–24). Sometimes the way the Lord accomplishes something in these passages is by sending an angel to do the task. That is why Moses can say that the Lord will bring the people into the land (6:8; 13:5) and that an angel will go before them to bring them to the land (23:20, 23). The angel is one means by which God directs the people to the land. Moses is another (33:12).

This does not mean that Moses is the Lord or that the Lord is an angel. It means God's direction is mediated through the work or presence of an intermediary. This is part of what Stephen means in Acts 7 when he says an angel spoke to Moses on Mount Sinai (Acts 7:38). The same teaching is reflected by Paul when he writes in Galatians that "the law was put into effect through angels by means of a mediator" (Gal. 3:19) as well as when the author of Hebrews 2:2 writes, "the message spoken through angels." These passages reflect the teaching of Moses in Deuteronomy 33:2, that the giving of the law was attended by the host of heaven.

To say that an angel can speak for God is different from saying the angel is God, just as a prophet can speak for God without being God. That is why the prophetic writers are careful to distinguish between God and the host of heaven, who are his creatures—not his coregents or equals. Recall that the fundamental distinction of the Christian worldview is that there is God and there is everything else. Angels are part of everything else, just as we are. We need to be careful not to make them more than they are.

Numbers

The angels make their next major appearance in the book of Numbers, conspicuously surrounding the messianic oracles of the prophet Balaam. God sends an angel to get the attention of the prophet beginning in Numbers 22:22. The angel stands in front of Balaam's donkey as he is riding and prevents the creature from moving forward. This happens three times, angering Balaam, who strikes the animal each time with his staff. In Numbers 28:22, we read that the Lord enables the donkey to complain to Balaam, and the two have a brief conversation, at which point "the LORD opened Balaam's eyes, and he saw the angel of the LORD" (Num. 22:31). This causes Balaam to fall to the ground. The angel repeats the donkey's question and informs Balaam that he has come out to oppose Balaam. In fact, the angel tells Balaam that the donkey saved his life by turning away (22:33).

Balaam replies by acknowledging his sin and offering to turn back the other way on the road. However, the angel tells Balaam that he can proceed on his way but should only say the words the angel tells him to say. Balaam accepts this arrangement, for, as he tells Balak, he will only speak the words God puts in his mouth (22:38).

In the next chapters, his oracles reflect what God had promised for his people and not the words of cursing that Balak had paid him to say. Here we have an angel delivering a message to a prophet and warning of the judgment God will bring against any false prophecy (motif 5). These are both standard motifs of angelic activity in Holy Scripture, as we have seen.

Deuteronomy

The angels do not play a major role in either Leviticus or Deuteronomy. But one passage in Deuteronomy is worth a quick mention.

In Deuteronomy 32:8, most ancient Greek versions of the Old Testament (often called the Septuagint or LXX) say that God fixed the borders of the peoples according to the number of "angels of God" (*angelon theou*). This reading is sometimes used as a basis for talking about territorial spirits. I'll discuss territorial spirits a bit more in a later chapter, but for now we can talk just about this text. The Greek versions of the Old Testament are translations of an earlier Hebrew version. In some cases, the translators work more or less word for word in their translation. In other cases, they freely add or expand to give their sense of the idea of the original. The same thing happens in our English translations. This verse is an example where the majority of the Greek manuscripts freely expand the sense of the original. The difference is that the Greek versions supply a word that does not appear in any Hebrew text.

You see, our oldest Hebrew version of this text (called 4QDeutj) does not contain the word *angels*. Instead, the oldest version says "sons of God." Two ancient Greek translations of this document read *huious theou*, which is a literal translation ("sons of God"). Most Greek translations, however, substitute the Hebrew word "sons" (*bene*) for the Greek word "angels" (*angelos*). Obviously, as a translation, this is a mistake because the word *son* doesn't mean "angel." Why then did those early Greek translators do this?

The translators are probably thinking of the phrase "sons of God" in Job (for example, Job 1:6) where the phrase does refer to angels. When they read that phrase in Deuteronomy 32:8, they think, *Aha! This refers to angels*, so they write the word *angel*. It may help you to know also that the community that produced the majority of the Greek translations of Deuteronomy was a group we know from other documents had an overly developed angelology. Angels served for them as an explanation for the presence of evil in the world as well as intermediaries necessary to know spiritual truths and a whole host of other ideas that were developed in the melting pot of Jewish religion and Greek philosophy. They had angels on the brain, so to speak. This explains why groups of people believed this text referred to angels and, perhaps, translated accordingly. However, all that tells us is something interesting about them and what they believed. It does not tell us what Moses meant.

Even if (for whatever reason) the translator thought the whole phrase "sons of God" really meant angels, then we would expect the whole phrase to be replaced by the single word *angels*. But we do not find that. Instead, we find only the word "sons" replaced. That helps explain why critical editions of the Septuagint of Deuteronomy usually read "sons of God" in Greek. The idea is that "angels" is a theological interpretation and not a translation. That is why nearly all English translations do not say "angels."

In contrast to the Greek readings, later Hebrew traditions do not mention angels at all. They take the phrase "sons of God" to refer to the people of Israel, which is the reason older English translations will read "sons" or "children" of Israel. "Sons of Israel" is also a legitimate way to understand the phrase "sons of God," since Israel is known as God's son in the Bible.

Well, you may be thinking, that is . . . a lot. What does the text really say?

Newer translations usually read "sons of God" because that reflects a more transparent rendering of our best evidence. That still leaves a further question, however: to whom or to what does the phrase "sons of God" refer? Unless one imports later Greco-Jewish ideas from non-biblical texts, there is no good reason to think the phrase means angels. But notice this: even if "angels" was correct, it would be a quick peek behind the scenes because that is where angels usually dwell—some version perhaps of motif 2.

The Motifs of Scripture

In our survey of the Book of Moses, we have seen that:

1. Angels worship the living God (as all creatures should) (Gen. 28).
2. Angels protect or guide a key figure in a Bible story (Gen. 24).
3. Angels announce or execute God's judgment (Num. 23).
4. Angels announce a significant birth (Gen. 16).
5. Angels deliver a message to someone or interpret a message to a prophet (Exod. 3).

This series of activities continues through the rest of the Bible and establishes the paradigm of expectation for Christians about what angels are and what they do. In other words, when the Bible speaks about angels, these five things are the sort of works we see them doing every time.

CHAPTER 3

ANGELS IN THE FORMER PROPHETS

You probably still have lots of questions about angels based on different things you may have heard or read. To be honest, you will probably still have questions at the end of this book. What I am trying to do here is to set up some guardrails for our thinking about the angels. Those guardrails ought to be based on what the Bible says, as accurately as we can understand it. So we are surveying the places in the Bible in which the word *angel* (*malak; angelos*) appears. We started with Genesis through Deuteronomy because the Book of Moses is foundational for the Bible and for Christian theology. That portion of our survey sets up our expectations of later inspired authors, and it lays the framework for our most crucial doctrines. This is true whether we are discussing creation, mankind, sin, God, or salvation.

It is also true for angelology. Remember that our worldview about angels should be crafted in submission to biblical authority. Our angelology, therefore, should have the pattern and proportion we find in Holy Scripture: not the pattern and proportion in other religions, contemporary media, the ancient Near East, the modern global South, Wall Street, the academy, the suburbs, or any other extrabiblical source. Scripture is to be our guide for understanding the spiritual realm. Although Christianity is a supernatural religion, it is not a superstitious one. The prophets and apostles—under the inspiration of the Holy Spirit—tell us what we need to know.

The pattern of angelic activity that we have seen in Moses's five books continues whenever angels appear through the rest of the books of the Old Testament and, indeed, the whole Bible. In this chapter, I will show where those patterns emerge in the books of the Former Prophets. We will find that angels do not play a major role in the Old Testament. Maybe that is already clear. Please note: that is not to say they do not exist or they are insignificant. But the proportion of teaching about angels is small relative to other doctrines. In fact, the proportion of mention is small. For now, I will pass over most instances of evil spirits because that subject will be covered in the later chapter on demons.

Former Prophets

The books called the Former Prophets are what you probably think of as most of the history books in your Bible: Joshua, Judges, 1 and 2 Samuel, and 1 and 2 Kings. These books tell the story of the failure of the people of Israel to show faithfulness to God and of their subsequent trials and tribulations—oppression, political fracture, and the division and destruction of their kingdom.

The source of these misfortunes is the idolatry of the people: their refusal to show sole allegiance to God and be faithful to his covenant and to listen to his prophets. As a result, the threatened punishments of breaching their promises (Lev. 26) fall on their heads. Nevertheless, God is faithful; indeed, he is gracious to provide for the people and maintain the line of descent that will ultimately lead to the Savior, Jesus Christ. That is the big idea of these books: they provide the historical and narrative background for understanding the message of the prophets, for they, too, are the message of the prophets.

In light of that, discussing the appearance of the angels in these texts is necessarily a secondary task. I say this to reiterate a point I have already made more than once. It is only to the extent that angelic activity is useful to the author's purposes in a given passage that he will mention them at all. The angels remain in these narratives secondary and background characters. But they do occasionally play a role, and understanding that role is worthwhile.

A word about organization: for the sake of space, I am planning to discuss the angels in light of the motifs we discovered in the Book of Moses, even though those are categories we crafted to help make sense of the big picture on angels—as opposed to categories Holy Scripture lays out for us in some kind of chart. The Bible isn't a textbook; it is a book of texts.

Note that the biblical authors can refer to angels without using the word *malak*—even though that is the most common word. One cannot merely do a word study and expect to find a system or to understand the texts in which the word appears. But none of the passages in which the authors use a different term significantly affect the pattern of motifs we discovered in Moses. We begin with an example of that scenario in the book of Joshua.

Joshua

In Joshua 5:13–15, we find the first instance of a heavenly creature in the book of Joshua. This angel announces himself to Joshua as the "commander of the LORD's army." Although Joshua does not use the word *malak* here (he says *ish*, which is a word for man), the pattern in the story was already established in Exodus 3. Furthermore, the image of a man with a drawn sword is common in Moses to identify an angel for the reader (see Num. 22:23–31). It will be used in later books as well (e.g., 1 Chron. 21:16). In Exodus 3, an angel appeared to Moses to give God's instructions and guidance in Moses's new role as leader of the people of Israel. In the first several chapters of Joshua, the author shows us that Joshua is taking over for Moses and filling the same role. One of the ways he does that is by highlighting times when Joshua did the same things Moses had done previously.

Hence, just as Moses encountered an angel who told him of God's plans (Exod. 3), so Joshua also experiences the same encounter before the battle at Jericho (Josh. 5). The author's signal that Joshua is serving as the new Moses is found in the repetition of the sentence, "Remove the sandals from your feet, for the place where you are standing is holy" (v. 15). This scene is a way to show (1) God's favor with Joshua, anticipating the success of the destruction of Jericho, and (2) that Joshua is fulfilling the role assigned to him just as Moses did.

Notice that the two men come to share a title. At the beginning of Joshua, we read that, after Moses's death, Moses is called "the LORD's servant" (e.g., Josh. 1:1), but by the end of the book, after Joshua's death, Joshua is called by the same title (Josh. 24:29). One feature of the book of Joshua is to show how and to what extent his generation was faithful in obeying Moses's instructions. The fact that Joshua fulfills his role well is part of the program. This instance of angelic appearance—a version of motif 5—is a way of highlighting that Joshua is a significant figure—in fact, a leader like Moses.

The only other appearances of *malakim* in Joshua are human messengers (Josh. 6:17–25; 7:22). As I noted earlier, the angels are minor players in Holy Scripture. They are real, and they are there; but we need to keep them in the right place and proportion in our thinking. The appearance of angelic figures is more frequent in Judges than in Joshua, however. In part, that is because the people increasingly find themselves distant from God and less clear on how to understand him or what he wants.

Judges

In Judges, the angelic figures appear in key moments to deliver messages, just as the prophets do. In fact, they perform the same function as the prophets in the author's organization of the book. Judges contains a series of cycles of apostasy, judgment, and rescue. The majority of the book is concerned with these cycles: the generations after Joshua fail to remember the Lord and commit idolatry by worshipping the gods of pagan peoples instead.

The corruption is so profound that even the judges are implicated, which the author indicates with the highly negative portrayal he provides for most of the figures in the book. The author of Judges shows that no matter how the word of God comes to the people—whether introduced through a prophet woman (Judg. 4:4), a prophet man (6:8), an angel (6:11), or the Lord (10:11)—their reaction is the same. They fail to be wholehearted toward the Lord, and they soon abandon any semblance of repentance they offer. Hence, in light of the author's purpose, the role of angels is the same as the role of the prophets: to deliver God's message to the people. We see the angels engaged in this work in chapters 2, 6, and 13.

The angel of the Lord comes from Gilgal to Bochim in chapter 2 and reminds the people that God had led them from Egypt and brought them into the land of the covenant. However, because the people did not obey the Lord, the angel says that God will no longer drive the people of the land out from before the people of Israel. The people weep at Bochim (which means "weeping" in Hebrew). In this instance, we see an example of motif 3—an angel speaking judgment over the people—but the message is also consistent with the pattern in the rest of the cycles.

In chapter 6, an angel again comes to speak on behalf of the Lord (motif 5). The angel appears to Gideon and addresses him, telling him that the Lord will be with

Gideon. But Gideon (addressing the angel as "sir" [HCSB]) asks why such bad things have befallen the people if it is true that the Lord is with them. At this point, the author drops the phrase "the angel" and expresses what follows as the Lord's words to Gideon. He can do this because the words of the angel are the words of the Lord—the very message the Lord sent the angel to deliver. After the Lord's message has been delivered, Gideon asks the angel to wait so that he can make an offering. However, like his people at the time in general, Gideon has forgotten how to worship the Lord. The angel gives him instructions for how to arrange the offering on a rock. Then the angel touches the offering with his staff causing fire to consume the offering. Finally, the angel departs from Gideon's sight. Although there is nothing remarkable about the verb here ("depart"), something about the experience strikes Gideon. He realizes, now after the fact, that he had been speaking to an angel. He cries out to God in despair because he perceives that he has seen the angel face-to-face. The Lord tells him not to worry.

Gideon, like many characters of Scripture, was not able to tell whether the angel was an angel or a man. Angels often appear indistinguishable from human messengers. As we have seen, the biblical languages even use the same word for both. Gideon also does not know enough about the Lord to understand how he should have reacted to the presence of one of the Lord's messengers. But we (the readers) do know that the angel is not a man; he is a celestial messenger. Because we have the witness of the prophets, we are in a better position to understand what is happening than a character like Gideon. This is why Peter praises Holy Scripture in the way he does (2 Pet. 1:19–21).

In chapter 13, there is a similar scene to chapter 6 involving an angel and Samson's parents (motif 4). In fact, we find the same confusion and ambiguity as in chapter 6. Samson's parents do not know if the messenger is a man, an angel, or even God. They do not seem to recognize that he is a celestial being until after he departs. However, Manoah does not cry out, as Gideon did, because he has seen one of God's angels. Instead, he laments because he believes he has seen God himself. Again, Manoah does not know enough about the Lord to understand how he should have reacted to the presence of one of the Lord's messengers. And, again, we (the readers) know that the angel is not the Lord; he is merely a celestial messenger. This highlights a feature of this part of the story: namely, that Manoah is clueless about God or God's ways. In fact, his wife explains that the Lord would not have shown the two of them "these things"—meaning the fire and the angel—if he had intended merely to kill them. In fact, the Lord had "now" spoken to them his words through the angel. They would find out in short order what the angel had promised about their son was true. In fact, this kind of announcement will be mirrored in the announcement the angel of the Lord makes to Mary about the birth of Jesus Christ.

Samuel–Kings

The instances of angelic appearance in these books are few and far between. In 1 and 2 Samuel, there are a handful of examples of humans speaking about angels, using them as a point of comparison (1 Sam. 29:9; 2 Sam. 4:17, 20; 2 Sam. 19:27). These texts show us that the characters in the story believed angels to be powerful and wise. However, they do not tell us what the author's perspective is, nor do they show the angels as agents or actors. Ultimately, the only perspective we care about is the author's—not the characters or the surrounding cultures or other elements—because only the author is inspired by God.

Now, we do find a scene of divine judgment in 2 Samuel 24 (motif 3). David is provoked by worry of his surrounding enemies to count up the total of fighting men he has at his disposal. After he receives the results, he realizes he has sinned. The prophet Gad offers David a choice of punishments from the Lord. David selects a plague to be on the people for three days. The Lord sends an angel to oversee the plague, but the Lord prevents the angel from affecting Jerusalem. The angel is over the threshing floor of Arunah when he ceases his destruction of the people. That location ends up being the place where David is instructed to offer a sacrifice to the Lord. It is important for the story of David in 1 and 2 Samuel that he does not take the threshing floor but rather insists on paying the correct price. This shows the contrast between his attitude with Bathsheba and his posture of repentance before the Lord here at the end of the book. Compared with this larger purpose of the author in these books, the details about the angel are purely incidental. The Chronicler will relate this story in more detail in a later book.

The books of 1 and 2 Kings similarly do not contain much about the angels. In 1 Kings 13:18, for instance, an old prophet tells a man of God that he had received a message from one of God's angels. The old prophet is lying, for he had not. Because the man of God listens to the false prophet, he violates the command God had already given him. He should have known not to trust the word of a prophet—even the word of an angel—that contradicted what God had said (a point Paul will emphasize with some force in Gal. 1:8). Likewise, we should not believe someone's teaching, advice, or counsel on any spiritual matter to the extent that it deviates from the Bible. Someone who claims to have spoken to a spiritual being deserves more scrutiny, not less.

In 1 Kings 19, an angel comes to instruct Elijah to eat when Elijah has given up on living. This happens twice in the passage (vv. 5–8). Because of the ministry of the angel, Elijah is revived and goes on his way. This is a brief example of motif 2. In 2 Kings 1, an angel comes to Elijah again to give him instructions on what to say to the messengers of the king of Samaria (v. 3). The angel also encourages him in this task, continuing the guidance motif (v. 15).

In 1 Kings 22, Jehoshaphat and the king of Israel are deciding whether they will go fight a battle at Ramoth-gilead. Most of the prophets of the court encouraged the kings to go ahead. Zedekiah even went so far as to make iron horns as a prophetic sign that the kings would have a victory in the battle. However, one of the prophets, Micaiah, had a reputation with the king of Israel for being a naysayer. So, when the kings send a messenger to bring Micaiah to the court, the man tells him that he needs to agree with the other prophets. However, Micaiah indicates that he will say whatever the Lord tells him to say instead.

In fact, initially he tells the king that the Lord will hand over Ramoth-gilead to him. But the king suspects that Micaiah is merely telling him what he wants to hear. So he insists that Micaiah tell the truth. Micaiah then offers an authentic prophecy, which bodes ill for the kings. He also tells of a vision he had. In the vision he saw the Lord enthroned in the presence of all the host of heaven. The writer does not use the word *malak* here, but elsewhere in Scripture the host of heaven are God's holy angels. The

Lord asks the angels which of them will trick the king into attacking Ramoth-gilead. The angels discuss among themselves before one of them agrees to do it. The Lord asks the angel how the angel plans to trick the king. The angel says that he will be a lying spirit in the mouth of the king's prophets. The Lord tells the angel that he should trick the king and he will succeed.

Micaiah relays an account of his vision to the king and informs him that the Lord has declared disaster against him by putting a lying spirit in the mouth of all his other prophets. Ultimately, Micaiah's word proves true, and hence he is confirmed as a true prophet according to Moses's standards from the book of Deuteronomy. The angels serve to execute God's judgment against the king (motif 4), but notice that it is the prophet who explains God's actions to the king. In fact, we see angels delivering messages to the prophets frequently (1 Kings 1:15), but the prophets are the center of focus. The fact that the angel delivers a message to the prophet or interprets a prophetic vision for him (motif 5) is an important literary feature. The biblical author uses that motif to show us that the prophet is a true prophet of God. Micaiah's authority as a prophet is also established in contrast to the false prophets of the kings in that he has seen into God's throne room. But the real sign of his authority is that the word he speaks comes true. After all, we already know from 1 Kings 13 that claiming to have encountered an angel is a simple thing to lie about, especially because it can be powerfully persuasive.

The final example in Kings is found in 2 Kings 19:35 when an angel destroys the camp of the Assyrians. This scene is another example of an angel executing God's judgment (motif 3). It also clearly displays the incredible power of the angels: one angel strikes down 185,000 Assyrians.

In each of these instances, the angels are supporting or defending God's prophet in his ministry before the Lord. In other words, they are supporting the delivery of God's messages. The fact that Elijah and Elisha are spoken to or guided or protected by angels at various times signals that they are remarkable figures in God's plan and that they have been set apart for his purposes. We know this from the reading because the appearances of angels are so rare that false prophets will lie about them to garner trust and to deceive the faithful.

This idea is consistent in the Scripture. Remember that Paul can say, "But even if we or an angel from heaven should preach to you a gospel contrary to what we have preached to you, a curse be on him!" (Gal. 1:8). The angels do not often interact with people in Scripture. In fact, when they do, it is a clue that those people are significant in God's plans. Hence, such appearances are uncommon by definition. Nevertheless, as we will see, when they do appear in Scripture it is to highlight something important.

CHAPTER 4

ANGELS IN THE LATTER PROPHETS

S tudents who knock on my office door usually appear timid as they peer through the window. In fact, many of them look embarrassed to be bothering me. Of course, they aren't bothering me. I'm there to be interrupted by their questions about life, jobs, marriage, sin, repentance, tragedy, triumph, or whatever bizarre excuse they have for not reading the book I assigned them. Sometimes they ask me about angels. Usually, I reply, "No, not really," encourage them to stop listening to that particular podcast or radio show or paperback novel or whatever, and that's it. But sometimes they are not coming to ask about angels in the abstract. Sometimes they want to talk about an angel they have seen themselves. Okay, usually, it is an angel their friend has seen.

I have a default response to these stories: your friend is probably mistaken. The reason is that your friend is not that important. Students don't particularly like hearing that (I imagine most people don't), but it is true. I have to clarify, "I did not say your friend was not important. I said that your friend is not *that* important." That *that* does some serious work here. In the Bible, angels do not appear willy-nilly to any person who happens to be in an unusual situation. As we have seen, they hardly appear at all. Yet a shocking number of my students have heard from friends who have seen angels. Here are the usual details of those stories: (1) the friend was on a trip in a foreign place (think South and East of where they normally live), (2) there were not many Christians in those places, and (3) the angel did not deliver a message. In fact, the angel usually just appears, and that's it. If you hear that kind of vague story often enough, you might begin to think it was true. But that script is different from the one in the Bible.

If we rely on the patterns in Scripture, we should think these contemporary stories are false. No motif in the Bible fits any of the patterns of these stories. If the Bible is our guide, then its patterns should shape our judgments and our expectations. You are not denying the supernatural reality of our world by declining to believe every sensational story you hear, even if the person telling you the story is earnest.

Why? Because experience is not self-interpreting.

Think about the number of times you have been disappointed. Every one of those times occurred because you thought something was going to happen, and it didn't. You expected one thing to happen, and you were wrong. We are not always good at guessing what will happen next.

Have you ever looked in the mirror and thought, *Yikes. I'm that thing there looking back at me?* Have you ever discovered that the party was really at 6:00 p.m. even though you just knew it was at 5:30? When it comes to mundane aspects of our own lives, we are often not clear-eyed witnesses. Why assume our insight is suddenly beyond criticism or investigation when it is about angels?

Remember, even when the angels appear to people in Holy Scripture, the people often do not recognize them. The author of Hebrews says, "Don't neglect to show hospitality, for by doing this some have welcomed angels as guests without knowing it" (Heb. 13:2).

I have said that angels appear at key moments to key people. Their presence highlights moments of significance in the biblical storyline: major births, major prophecies, major judgments, and so on. This continues to be the role they play in the so-called Major Prophets: Isaiah, Jeremiah, and Ezekiel. The script continues in the Minor

Prophets: Hosea, Joel, Amos, Obadiah, Jonah, Micah, Nahum, Habakkuk, Zephaniah, Haggai, Zechariah, and Malachi.

Major and *Minor* refer only to the relative size of the books. The books are both Christological and eschatological. That means they look forward to the coming Messiah, Jesus Christ, and to his eternal, victorious reign at the end of time. They do this by using contemporary examples of sin, repentance, salvation, and judgment as emblems or signs of what God will do through Christ in the latter days. Hence, these books have ongoing relevance; they are not merely the ruminations of an ancient vision of reality. They speak to the perennial human concerns of God's people according to a family of texts and images that we are to read and remember. Amid these books we have both prophetic utterances and their explanations as well as narrative accounts from the lives of the prophets that help illustrate the message and meaning these inspired books hold for us. Like the *history* books of the former prophets, these books are a living word for us today.

As with the Former Prophets, the angelic figures who appear in these books do so according to the same set of literary motifs Moses provided. Furthermore, the angels remain background figures, even in instances where the descriptions of the prophets tend to provoke in contemporary writers a mistaken instinct to elaborate what the book says or to construct imaginative details about angelic presence and activity. A vivid description in the Prophets is not license for us to elaborate what they say and add new colors and ideas from a variety of external sources. We must be constrained by the force of the prophets' message because their message is the divinely appointed way we can know what God wants us to know. Hence, even though our subject will cause us to focus on the angels with special emphasis, we should not lose sight of the fact that the books' meaning has been determined by their authors. Lastly, we can easily discuss all the angelic appearances in the whole Bible in a relatively short space within a short book.

Isaiah

The most famous angels in Isaiah's book—probably the most famous angels of the Old Testament—are never called angels by the prophet. Instead, they are called seraphim, and they appear for the only time in Holy Scriptures in chapter 6 of Isaiah. These celestial beings are depicted in the worship of God in heaven, flying or floating around his throne and declaring his praises by celebrating his holiness and his glory. The visual description of these beings is strange. They were "standing above him; they each had six wings: with two they covered their faces, with two they covered their feet, and with two they flew" (Isa. 6:2). As they fly, they call out to one another about God's glory: "Holy, Holy, Holy is the LORD of Armies; his glory fills the whole earth" (6:3). "Armies" or "Hosts" often refers to the host of heaven in Hebrew, the "army" of angels that serve God in heaven and on earth. We saw this description in 1 Kings 22. The voices of the seraphim shake the foundations of the temple doorways in Isaiah's vision (6:4).

One of the seraphim takes a coal from the altar with tongs and then touches that coal to Isaiah's lips, thus preparing Isaiah for his prophetic ministry (Exod. 4:10; Jer. 1:7). The seraph tells Isaiah that because the coal has touched his lips his sins are atoned for (Isa. 6:6–7). Presumably this is because of Isaiah's confession of sins and his inadequacy before God (Isa. 6:5). In this scene we see celestial beings worshipping God (motif 1) as well as an angel serving to prepare a prophet for his ministry (motif 5).

This presentation is in keeping with the general structure of the book of Isaiah. Let's remember that Scripture does not contain independent teaching units on the angels, nor do the authors simply toss them in because of some ancient worldview. The authors mention the angels when it is relevant to the story they are writing through the inspiration of the Holy Spirit. The mention and description of the angels, then, often serves the literary purposes of signaling to the reader that God is doing or saying something important. This is the idea of divine theme music we first encountered in Exodus and Joshua.

Many instances of the angels are introduced with *hinneh* (Hebrew) or *idou* (Greek)—words that mean "Behold!" or "Look!" or "Pay attention!" In Ezekiel, for example, we will see an elaborate description of angelic beings as a literary introduction to Ezekiel's message. However, there are other times when an angelic appearance is not announced at all. The angel or angels merely appear and do their set task. We have seen literary examples of this technique already in Genesis 18. Isaiah uses the same technique in his book.

For example, in Isaiah 37, an angel is sent to defeat the Assyrian army. He is God's means of fulfilling the judgment God spoke over the king of Assyria (Isa. 37:33–35). After the Lord says that he will defend his city, an angel kills 185,000 Assyrians at their encampment. This is the same story relayed to us in 1 Kings. When King Sennacherib discovers all the dead bodies in the morning, he returns home to Nineveh. This is a clear instance of motif 3: God sent an angel to destroy the enemy army. But the whole gory business is described in verse 36. There is no fanfare because the destruction happens at night and because the word of the Lord has already come to the king through the prophet.

I have said to you (so much so that you may think, *Yes, yes, get on with it!*) that *the angels are usually behind the scenes, and their appearances are rare.* Consider that the angels do not play a significant role in the book of Jeremiah. In fact, the word *malak* appears only one time in the whole book, and, in that instance, it refers to human messengers.

Ezekiel

In Ezekiel, by contrast, we are presented with celestial beings who are described as living creatures (Ezek. 1:5). The function they play is to identify the significance of the prophet Ezekiel and to introduce the reader to the divine nature of Ezekiel's prophecy in the rest of the book. The description of these creatures (later identified as cherubim in Ezek. 10) is bizarre. In fact, when they appear again in Holy Scripture, John describes them a bit differently from Ezekiel (Rev. 4:6–8). This difference does not mean Ezekiel was right about the description and John was wrong: both men describe what they see under the inspiration of the Holy Spirit. The difficulty of capturing the vision in words testifies to the otherness of these creatures. It also indicates the folly of trying to find out about them on our own. As we have seen, the prophets do not always understand the meaning of what they see at first glance. As with angelic appearances in the past, the cherubim let you know that the real show is about to begin.

> I looked, and there was a whirlwind coming from the north, a huge cloud with fire flashing back and forth and brilliant light all around it. In the center of the fire, there was a gleam like amber. The likeness of four living creatures came from it, and this was their appearance: They looked something like a human, but each of them had four faces and four wings. Their legs were straight, and the soles of their feet were like the hooves of a calf, sparkling like the gleam of polished bronze. They had human hands under their wings on their four sides. All four of them had faces and wings. Their wings were touching. The creatures did not turn as they moved; each one went straight ahead. Their faces looked something like the face of a human, and each of the four had the face of a lion on the right, the face of an ox on the left, and the face of an eagle. That is what their faces were like. Their wings were spread upward; each had two wings touching that of another and two wings covering its

body. Each creature went straight ahead.
(Ezek. 1:4–12)

The image here is so vivid and strange that it is difficult to imagine. In fact, the four faces of the creatures were appropriated by later Christian artists as images for each of the four Gospel writers. Matthew was depicted as a human because of his focus on the incarnation; Mark as a lion because of the boldness of his preaching; Luke as an ox because of his focus on the temple; and John as an eagle because of his emphasis on the deity of Jesus.[1] In contrast, cherubim are typically depicted today as chubby white children with tiny wings. This symbol has a long history, but its goal is not to represent the cherubim as they actually appeared to Ezekiel.

When Christian artists were looking for a typically Greco-Roman image of a celestial messenger to use in their visual art, the image available was a depiction of Hermes or Cupid—a messenger "god" of the Greco-Roman pantheon. Since angels are messengers in Holy Scripture, this drawing seemed to many Christian artists like an appropriate one to borrow in their paintings and mosaics. In fact, in a gallery of seventeenth-century art, you might find a traditional depiction of a Greco-Roman myth that included a painting of Cupid placed next to a painting depicting a biblical scene in which the "Cupid" figure is clearly a representation of an angel. The artistic technique represents a critical assimilation of an artistic idea. But it would be a mistake to think these images are in fact what angels look like, if we are relying on the Bible for our understanding.

Ezekiel is not appropriating a prior vision of an angelic being, however. He is describing what he sees (Ezek. 1:1–2). This is the important point: not that angels are weird and fantastic but that the angels precede a description of one seated on a throne. The seated one gleams like amber (similar to the initial appearance of the cherubim) but also like fire and with a brilliant light like the bow in the heavens (1:27–28). This shows that the figure on the throne is greater than the strange creatures that preceded him in the vision. After all, when the voice comes from above the cherubim, they stop flying and lower their wings (1:25). It is not until the appearance of the glory of the Lord that Ezekiel falls to the ground (1:28). The angels, strange and eerie as they may be, are merely an announcement that precedes the presence of God. This is similar to how the vision of the angel in the bush preceded the voice of God to Moses, or the vision of the seraphim preceded the voice of God to Isaiah. The host of heaven are not God's equals or vice-regents. They are his messengers. Remember the only two categories are God and everything else. Here, as often in Scripture, they announce his presence to a prophet (motif 5). Notice that the sound of the presence of the angels accompanies Ezekiel's departure to speak to the exiles (3:13), but we are not given a further description of them until later in the book.

Even then, in chapter 10, the cherubim are described in largely similar terms to the way they are described in chapter 1. Ezekiel is keen to repeat that the creatures he sees in the later vision are the same ones he had seen at the beginning (10:15, 20–22). In chapter 10, Ezekiel sees the glory of the Lord leave from its presence over the carved cherubim of the altar (10:4) to sit upon the four cherubim who hover above the threshold (10:18). After the prophecy of the next chapter, the cherubim move to a mountain east of the city, and the glory of the Lord goes with them (11:23). The presence of the cherubim showcases and introduces the presence of the Lord, and he travels upon them and their "wheels" (1:15–21; 11:22) as if riding a chariot away from the city. In this passage, they are at once helping communicate a vision to Ezekiel (motif 5) and announcing judgment on the people for their idolatry (motif 3).

In similar vein, in Ezekiel's final vision of a restored temple, a figure—a "man"—appearing like bronze shows him the measurements of the new temple. The man tells him that Ezekiel has been brought to the temple "so that I might show it to you" (40:4). The Lord brings Ezekiel to the place of the vision (40:1) so that an angelic figure can translate the message to the prophet for the people to receive: "Report everything you see to the house of Israel" (40:4). The angel is a messenger to the prophet, who then relays the messages to us in Holy Scripture (motif 5).

The Twelve

In the twelve Minor Prophets, angels again are mentioned but do not play a significant role. In fact, in Joel, Amos, Obadiah, Jonah, Micah, Nahum, Habakkuk, Zephaniah, Haggai, and Malachi, angels are not mentioned. When the word *malak* appears in those books (in only two instances), it means messenger, not angel.

In Nahum, for example, the prophet says in 2:13 that the "sound of your messengers (*malakim*) will never be heard again." In Haggai, we find the phrase *malak Yahweh* (1:13), which is usually translated "the angel of the LORD," but, of course, that would be an inappropriate translation in Haggai because the phrase is used as a title for Haggai the prophet. That verse will be important when we consider the question of the angel of the Lord in chapter 9 of this book because it shows that *malak Yahweh* is not a title for one individual. In any case, angels are rare in the Minor Prophets.

Angels do appear in the books of Hosea and Zechariah, however. The single mention in Hosea is important, but it is also oblique. In Hosea 12:3–4, we read: "In the womb he grasped his brother's heel, and as an adult he wrestled with God [*Elohim*]. Jacob struggled with the angel [*malak*] and prevailed; he wept and sought his favor." This part of the prophecy of Hosea helps clarify what was happening in Genesis 32, as we previously discussed in chapter 2.

The word *God* (*elohim*) is used in parallel to the word *angel* (*malak*). That means the word *angel* is clarifying what the word *God* in the previous line means. In fact, the word *God* in Hebrew in this case is *elohim*, which is a plural word used to refer to false "gods," angels and spiritual beings, and human judges. So the word *angel* is being used to clarify that Jacob's wrestling was with an angel, not with God himself. Of course, none of this is the point of Hosea 12, the goal of which is to establish the relationship between the deceitfulness of the patriarch Jacob and the ongoing deceitfulness of his descendant people Israel.

The emphasis of Hosea on the faithlessness of the people is a major point of the book (see Hosea 4:2 and 10:4 for other examples). The reference to the angel with whom Jacob wrestled is merely part of a summary of major events of Jacob's life in Moses's account. Hence, this is a good example of how facts about angels are included in the Bible incidentally or with reference to some other subject.

The scenes in Zechariah, in contrast to Hosea, do not merely rehearse an earlier biblical story. Instead, we find that Zechariah's visions are interpreted to him by angels (motif 5). We will see a similar pattern in Daniel and in John's Revelation. The first of Zechariah's visions (1:8–17) is a good example of the pattern. Zechariah sees a "man" riding on a horse among myrtle trees. He also sees other horses with him. Zechariah does not understand what he is seeing, so he asks for an explanation (vv. 8–9). The man on the horse, who is an angel, explains that the horses are patrolling the earth. The man on the horse steps out of the scene, so to speak, to explain the vision. It would be like viewing an art gallery and wondering aloud what a painting was about only to have one of the characters in the painting step out and explain it to you. The point is that the vision needs an explanation, and the explanation we read about is the one Zechariah received from the angel.

This observation is important: the vision is so difficult to grasp that the prophet needs an interpreter. Hence, we should listen with tremendous caution when people tell us stories about angels and demons based on their own personal experience. The apostles and prophets prove to us that we are likely inadequate to understanding our supernatural experiences rightly, apart from Scripture. That is why God has graciously provided us an account of these things in Holy Scripture in black print on white paper (or tan papyrus as the case may be).

In the sequence of visions that occupy chapters 2 and 3 of Zechariah, the angel from the first vision reenters the "painting," and a different angel comes in his place to help Zechariah understand the visions (Zech. 2:3). The original angel returns in 4:1 and continues to help Zechariah understand the visions. All of these instances in Zechariah fall into the category of motif 5. Of course, the angels are not the point of the visions. The visions offer a Christological and eschatological summary of God's plan. But the angels are important features of the book because they explain to Zechariah what he is seeing. He, in turn, writes the whole account for us as he is inspired by God.

In the Major and Minor Prophets, we continue to see the same motifs or patterns of angelic activity. Those stories need to color our expectations and our vision of the supernatural world we live in. Those patterns need to establish how we judge angelic tales.

---

1. One example of this kind of artistic treatment may be found in/at https://digitalcollections.tcd.ie/concern/works/hm50tr726?locale=en.

CHAPTER 5

ANGELS IN THE
WISDOM BOOKS

I n this chapter, we will consider the angelic appearances in the remaining books of the Old Testament.
Many of these writings are Wisdom books; they
intend to tell God's people something about how to live his
way in his world. In so doing, they help us understand God
and his purposes by helping us make sense of the Scripture
as well as our place in the world. It is conspicuous, then,
that the angels (or demons) rarely appear in these books.
Why is it conspicuous? Because if angels and demons were
to be major features of Christian living, then we would
expect much more advice and instruction on how to deal
with them than Scripture provides.

Since the Bible is sufficient for the faith, life, and practice of God's people, we have to be careful to emphasize what it emphasizes. All the more in the didactic instruction of the New Testament, we will find that angels and demons are real creatures in God's world, but they are not major role players in Christian living—real but not major. Teaching that makes angels and demons central to the Bible's message is inconsonant with a fair reading of Holy Scripture.

For example, the word *malak* does not even appear in Ruth, Ezra, Esther, or the Song of Songs. It does appear once in Ecclesiastes 5:5 where it means messenger, not angel. Likewise, it appears once in plural in Nehemiah 6:3 where it means messengers, not angels. It occurs a whopping three times in Proverbs. In each case, it means messenger. The word does appear with the meaning *angel*, however, in Daniel, Psalms, Job, and 1 and 2 Chronicles. Of course, there are other ways the biblical authors can refer to angels, as we have seen already.

Even in the books of the Writings in which they do appear, most instances are poetic reflections (Psalms) or retellings (Chronicles) of events that were previously narrated earlier in the Bible. In Daniel the angels are more active, elaborating key moments of protection in the book and interpreting messages for Daniel. In Job the presence of angels assembled before the Lord serves as a frame of the narrative in the book. But aside from their depiction as present in the host of heaven, they are not major characters. Satan, by contrast, is a major figure in the framing of the book of Job, but a full consideration of the devil and his angels (Matt. 25:41) will wait for a later chapter.

Daniel

Daniel portrays the angels in several major scenes, but the motifs are the same as what we have seen before. Daniel 3 and 6 contain scenes in which an angel is sent by God to protect the major characters of the story. In the visions that conclude the book of Daniel, angels serve as interpreters for Daniel in much the same way they did for Zechariah.

Daniel 3 contains a famous story in which the pagan king Nebuchadnezzar makes an enormous idol and instructs the people to worship it. In the story Daniel's three faithful friends from chapter 1—Shadrach, Meshach, and Abednego—refuse to bow to the idol. The key point of the story is that they will have faith in God even if he chooses not to rescue them from the punishment they are facing. This is an important point because it cuts against retributive theology, which is a common view in most religions (and among some Christians) that God or spiritual forces immediately respond for your benefit when you act righteously and for your harm when you do not. That just isn't how the God of the Bible works.

The three men are thrown into a fiery furnace for their disobedience to the king. However, as the king looks into the fire, he is astonished to see four figures in it, not merely the three he had ordered thrown in. The fourth one "looks like a son of the gods" (v. 25). In Aramaic, this is *bar elahin*. Daniel contains sections in both Hebrew and Aramaic.

In some English translations, this phrase has unfortunately been translated "son of God" or (even worse) "Son of God" with a capital S. Neither of those translations is accurate, and both are potentially misleading. The word "god" is plural in Aramaic here. The phrase "son of the gods" is a common Aramaic way to refer to angels, false gods, or other celestial beings. An overwrought desire to help this text be more Christian (it is sufficiently Christian the way Daniel wrote it) has sometimes prompted translators to translate as if the figure were the eternal Son or Jesus, but that is simply false. Don't mistake me: this is not a modern agenda. Theodotion was trying it in the second century. The fact remains that we are a people of the Book. Our theology cannot say what the grammar does not support.

In fact, if you keep reading the story, Nebuchadnezzar praises the God of Shadrach, Meshach, and Abednego because he "sent his angel and rescued his servants who trusted in him" (v. 28). Here we find the Aramaic word *malak*. This is the same word as in Hebrew. It clarifies that the earlier phrase, *bar elahin*, uttered by the pagan king, meant "angel." The two words inform each other. This is exactly the same strategy we saw in Genesis 19 and Hosea 12, in which the author clarifies his meaning by using different terms. God sent an angel to protect the men in the fire (motif 2).

The same thing that happens to the three friends also happens to Daniel in chapter 6. The pagan king, Darius, has ordered that no one can pray to any god or man except himself for thirty days. Daniel refuses to comply with this immoral order, and he continues to pray according to his habit. When he is caught disobeying the king, he is thrown into a den of lions, even though the king does not want to punish him. In fact, the king himself prays that the God of Daniel will deliver him (v. 16). The king spends a restless night fasting.

When he returns in the morning, he calls to Daniel to see if Daniel's God has been able to rescue him. Daniel's response reveals that the same thing that happened to his friends has happened to him: God sent an angel to protect them from harm. "My God sent his angel and shut the lions' mouths; and they haven't harmed me" (v. 22). Of course, we are not promised protection from difficulties in life, but with these particular people God protects them by sending an angel (motif 2). In both cases, this rescue brings notoriety to God before the pagan kings. In fact, for Darius, the rescue is so moving that he makes a decree that everyone "must tremble . . . before the God of Daniel" (v. 26).

Of course, angels also interpret dreams and visions for Daniel in the book, an instance of motif 5. They also sometimes appear in the dreams of the kings. For example, Nebuchadnezzar has a dream in which he sees what he calls a "watcher" and a "holy one" descend from heaven (4:13). Those are both words that sometimes refer to angels. Daniel repeats the same words (4:23) when he interprets the dream, but the angel is not significant in the interpretation of the dream (4:24–26). Daniel's account of the dream comes true, at which point Nebuchadnezzar praises the God who does as he pleases with both "the army of heaven and the inhabitants of the earth" (4:35). The point of this episode was to humble the king before God (4:37), so the angels are incidental to the overall story. But we do see them active in the vision, much as we did in Zechariah.

In chapters 7–12, Daniel sees a series of visions, and there is generally a figure nearby—usually called a "man"—who interprets the vision for him. This first occurs in chapter 7:16: "I approached one of those who were standing by and asked him to clarify all this." In chapter 8,

Daniel recounts another vision he could not understand. A voice calls to a figure named Gabriel and commands him to explain the vision to Daniel (8:16). Daniel is terrified at this figure's approach (8:17). In chapter 9, we read that "Gabriel, the man I had seen in the first vision" (v. 21), returns to give Daniel further understanding. In this case Gabriel gives Daniel a message. It is essentially a message that affirms the words of the prophets and encourages Daniel that they will be ultimately fulfilled as God intended.

In chapter 10, Daniel has another encounter with another "man." This man is "dressed in linen, with a belt of gold from Uphaz around his waist. His body was like beryl, his face like the brilliance of lightning, his eyes like flaming torches, his arms and feet like the gleam of polished bronze, and the sound of his words like the sound of a multitude" (vv. 5–6).

In what follows, Daniel is told that the angelic figure had been sent by God to assist Daniel from the first day that he began fasting (10:2). However, he was prevented from arriving immediately because he was opposed by "the prince of the kingdom of Persia . . . for twenty-one days" (10:13). This is the length of time Daniel ended up fasting (10:2).

Apparently, this prince of Persia was able to prevent the angel messenger from arriving before then. The angel tells Daniel that Michael "one of the chief princes, came to help me after I had been left there with the kings of Persia" (10:13). We would love for the angel to elaborate a bit here! This is the first place in Scripture that we have read about conflict between angels. What we have are some tantalizing hints but no real substance.

Therefore, before we proceed, let's keep a few things in mind. The information about the "princes" is only given to Daniel to explain the delay and to reassure him that he has favor with God. The angel does not offer more information because Daniel doesn't need to know it, and neither do we. Our goal has to be understanding the message of Holy Scripture (Dan. 9:25). The incidental details certainly provoke questions of curiosity, and this seems only natural and right. But those questions can sometimes cause us to manufacture answers that have nothing to do with what God has revealed. We must be cautious about that threat. I do not want to be a killjoy, but the number of people who have used this suggestive text to manufacture bizarre stories is astonishing. Even the scholars are not immune to superstition here, and scholars are supposed to be sober minded, even boring.

The word *prince* or *princes* is a translation that has been borrowed from the King James Version, but the Hebrew word is more generic than *prince*. It usually means something more like "leader" or "captain." "Prince," it seems to me, sometimes gives readers the impression of more authority than these beings (whatever they are) really seem to have. What we have here are captains in some sort of conflict. Apparently, the angels are engaged with one another "behind the scenes" in a manner associated with different people groups or nations.

These are not "territorial spirits," since these creatures are not limited to any particular territory. Note that Michael, a prince of Daniel's people, is serving them even though Daniel's people are in exile. The insistence of territorial spirits that you sometimes read is an attempt to fill in the gaps of this story with information gleaned from other religions. In most animistic and most polytheistic religions, the gods or spirits are associated with particular locations. That pagan people had this view is found recorded in Holy Scripture (see 1 Kings 20), but this is not the view of the prophets and apostles. Espousing a view in territorial spirits has led to many syncretistic practices in global Christianity that are simply not endorsed or commanded anywhere in Holy Scripture.

Instead, what we can say is that some spiritual forces are associated with major nations or powers. That much is borne out by what follows in the text, and we will see some more reminders of that reality when we get to Paul (Eph. 6:10–20). But the angel's purpose is not to give us insight into those conflicts except as they have bearing on God's promises. They simply aren't our business. We certainly aren't expected to go searching for more information about them!

Let's recall that the purpose of chapter 10 is to introduce the last two chapters of the book of Daniel. To this point in Daniel, we have heard various prophecies about kings and the future. These appeared in chapters 2, 7, 8, and 9 but with gaps. In Daniel 10–12, Daniel records the whole sequence based on the message and interpretation the angel provides. Whatever conflicts are going on among the kings of the earth in the days to follow Daniel (or us), something related is happening unseen among the celestial host. As we already learned in Daniel, God does what he pleases "with the army of heaven and the inhabitants of the earth" (4:35). So Daniel is encouraged by the angel that the delay was not a lack of respect for Daniel but rather that a lot is going on. In spite of the conflicts among the angels, however, Daniel has favor with God, and the waiting of Daniel, it seems to me, is the appropriate posture for all Christians. After all, the message of the prophets is frequently that we must wait and hope on God's rescue. This is part of what the angel goes on to explain to Daniel.

The angel who is speaking to Daniel in chapter 10 was opposed by some other angels (perhaps demons) who are associated in some way with Persia. Michael, who is associated with the people of Israel, assisted him. After he finishes speaking with Daniel, the first angel will return to a conflict against the prince of Persia. After that (at some point), he will oppose the prince of Greece. These princes correspond to the first two nations mentioned in the prophecy that the angel brings to Daniel (11:2–4). Whatever these princes are, they are not gods, for the gods of the nations are idols of metal (11:8). Nevertheless, they may be called "gods" in Hebrew or Aramaic at times because those languages use *elohim* to refer to angels, gods, and men in a way that our English word *god* does not usually function. We usually use the phrase "false god"—either because the entity in question isn't even real or because the being pretends to be a god but is, in fact, a demon. As the sequence of kingdoms and nations comes and goes in anticipation of the day of the Lord, Michael will rise up near the end (12:1). After that, Daniel is given a promise of resurrection at the end of the days (12:2).

In Daniel we have confirmed that angels are involved in God's affairs without our knowledge. They are not merely delivering messages. We knew that anyway, but Daniel highlights the point for us vividly (though perhaps we wish he would say more!). But, as they pertain to us, we find that Daniel shares this information about them using only the same motifs we find time and again in the Bible. We need to be cautious not to manufacture hints about their business, however tantalizing, into the main theme of our reflections. A peek behind the curtain is not a backstage pass.

After all, we do not have to read books like Daniel on their own. We have the rest of Holy Scripture. The figure from Daniel that later writers make the most fuss about—draw the most attention to—is the figure of the "son of man," Jesus. Just in Matthew, look at Matthew 8:20; 9:6; 12:8; 19:28; 24:29–31; 25:31; or 26:63–64. The angels come up in some of those verses as well but as background characters in support of the star of the show, the Lord Jesus Christ.

Psalms and Chronicles

In Psalms, *malak* occurs only a handful of times. In Psalm 34, for example, the psalmist explains that an angel surrounded the contrite man (motif 2), and in Psalm 35, the angel is depicted in his execution of God's judgment against the wicked (motif 5). Nothing in these occurrences falls outside the motifs we have already seen. The angels are also mentioned occasionally using other words. God is frequently referred to as the Lord of hosts, for example: the one who is ruler of the armies of heaven. Of course, the angels are exhorted to worship God: "Praise him, all his angels; praise him, all his heavenly armies" (Ps. 148:2). I hold off on elaborating about a few of the psalms because they are referred to in the New Testament, and we will look at them in the following two chapters.

One last note in our study of the Old Testament: in 1 and 2 Chronicles, the angels appear in stories that are retellings from the Former Prophets. The Chronicles do not merely rehearse those earlier books; they have their own shape and emphasis. However, for our purposes, the texts refine or enhance our understanding of what the angels did in particular key moments. The texts in Chronicles are 1 Chronicles 21, which corresponds to 2 Samuel 24, and 2 Chronicles 32:21, which corresponds to 1 Kings 19.

What We've Learned in the Old Testament

Perhaps it is becoming clearer why I am a reluctant angelologist. If Scripture is to be our guide on these questions (and it is!), then there just isn't much we can say about angels. We have seen that each instance follows the established motifs from the first five books of the Bible. Angels are rarely discussed in the Old Testament, and, when they appear, they do so in regular and familiar ways. This is not to say angels are not majestic, frightening, or awe-inspiring. It certainly isn't to say that they aren't real.

Instead, there is an established pattern of what angels do and how we should understand their work based on what God has chosen to reveal in his book. Angels are messengers; they appear rarely to key people at key moments; they are background characters in God's plan. Nothing in the Old Testament teaches us to seek them out, invoke them, or concern ourselves with them at all. The prophets set up precisely zero expectation that you would ever encounter an angel. Even if you did, you probably would not realize it.

I've mentioned that I get lots of questions from students about angels and the concern I have about being a continual killjoy. After all, I'm not interested in taking anything away from my students. I just want to make sure they have their emphasis in the right place, that they are using a biblical script and pattern as the locus of their interpretations.

Still, I'm sometimes asked, "But wait! Can't angels do other things as well? I mean, isn't it possible?" I try to answer that question as gently as I can: "Maybe." However, that is really the wrong question. All kinds of things are possible. Deep-sea creatures, for example, that almost no one ever sees might do all kinds of interesting things. But, then again, why think so? And, perhaps to sharpen the point, why think they do any particular thing? Should anything about what they do affect how you live your life?

Stories about angels are a bit like fisherman tales. You might believe them if you knew the fisherman personally and it was clear enough from the context of his story that he wasn't exaggerating or caught up in the telling of the story or spinning a yarn because it is fun. Perhaps, your friend, Carl, the deep-sea fisherman, tells you a fascinating story about some rare and rarely seen beast of the depths. Something large and powerful and awe-inspiring. A great squid from the abyss perhaps—all tentacles and beak and great rolling eyes. Ah, the sound it made as it roared up from the waves! How could you not hope the tale was true? After all, isn't it wonderful to believe there is something great and wild in this boring world of concrete and transistor chips? His eyes grow wide as he recounts the tale, and you shudder a bit as you file away his tale in your memory to savor later. Whether he was telling the truth, lying, or the truth simply got bigger in the telling, ultimately it won't make much difference to a landlubber like you. But the very idea that hidden from our normal view there is something vibrant and alien and powerful is bracing, even seductive.

Angels are like that for some people. Hidden, powerful, intelligent creatures. Close by but unseen. To believe in them is to believe in a world that isn't all public transportation and parking meters and elevator rides. A world that isn't lawn mowing and car washes and AC repair.

But Christians already have a world like that.

We live in a world in which God created all things by speaking them into existence. A world in which the earth teems with all manner of bird and beast and creeping thing. A world full of people just like you with hopes and dreams, fear and regrets. A world, yes, with spiritual creatures we do not see. A world in which the Son of God became what you are—a human being—so that he might shed his real, human blood as a sacrifice for the sins of mankind. A world in which a man or woman can become an heir to the kingdom by trusting in God's message of salvation. A rich, vibrant, technicolor world. A world with all the beauty and terror of any fisherman tale.

There is an important difference between stories about angels and stories about other rarely sighted, mysterious material creatures: the Holy Scriptures tell us what to expect about angels by showing us key motifs about their action and interaction with mankind. Since we have this information already, speculation and fancy, however intriguing or fun, are simply the wrong posture. We aren't invited to an independent study of these things. We don't have the right equipment for the job. Angels are unseen creatures. They aren't herd animals or beasts over which we can assert our dominion or to which we can apply the scientific method.

If my grandmother tells me, "You won't believe it! Baby, I saw an angel in a shop window last week," I'll tell her that, surely, she saw her reflection. But, if she insists, I'm not going to be argumentative even though I think she is probably mistaken. Why not? Nothing stands or falls by it, even though nothing in the Scripture suggests angels appear recognizably in shop windows. She'll tell me, "I saw that angel, and I just knew God loved me." Praise God.

But suppose she starts telling me what the angel told her and how she needs to do such-and-such because he said whatever he said. Well, now, I'm going to have to lovingly insist that we pay more careful attention to the biblical witness about the angels. Even reviewing the Old Testament is enough to see that they are real, rare, and rarely involved in our affairs in ways we could recognize. In the next two chapters, we will see the New Testament confirm this initial impression.

CHAPTER 6

———

ANGELS IN THE
NEW TESTAMENT
NARRATIVES

L et's take stock. By the time we have read through the Old Testament, we have read 78 percent of the Bible. Very little of that has been about the angels, but they have cropped up from time to time. When they have, the writers have depicted them in similar ways. The angels only do a handful of things—at least, we are only told about a handful of the things they do. Those motifs, as I have called them, ought to serve as our guard-rails for thinking about the angels because the Bible should be our guide for spiritual things. In the Old Testament, we have found that the angels

1. Worship God.
2. Protect or guide key figures.
3. Announce or execute God's judgment.
4. Announce significant births.
5. Deliver or interpret messages to prophets.

In the New Testament, when we look for the word "angel" (*angelos*), we find the same patterns or motifs.

The New Testament does not divide as naturally as the Old Testament does because it was written in a shorter period of time. For our purposes, we are going to examine the writings of the New Testament in two big groups: the Gospel accounts and Acts, and the rest. There is nothing necessary about this arrangement, but it will make the material manageable for our purpose. Remember that our purpose is a secondary one: we want to find out what we can glean from the prophetic and apostolic witness about angels: those other moral, rational agents God created besides us. Of course, these passages still do not discuss the angels as a focal part of the story—they mention them. That is enough for what we need to know.

I want to head off a query I often get from students about angels and demons. Most people who are familiar at all with the Bible are familiar with the *stories* of the Gospel accounts and little else. But, while this familiarity is often with *stories*, it is not with *texts*. What do I mean by that? I mean they have a general sense of what happened or what parable Jesus told or what miracle he did, but they could not say where in the Bible the event was recorded or what purpose that particular miracle had in the context of (say) Matthew's book. In other words, we know a bunch of stories as basically independent histories from the earthly ministry of Jesus, but we do not see them as connected parts of Matthew, Mark, Luke, or John's attempt to tell one coherent story about the gospel of Jesus Christ, each man in his own way as he was carried along by the Holy Spirit. That distinction may not sound too important, but it is a distinction that makes a big difference in your Bible reading.

After all, our goal in Bible reading is to listen to what the author said, not to interrupt him to clarify everything he says with reference to our doctrines or what is written in some other place. Certainly, we should not interrupt him to clarify what he says with reference to what pagan people believed or believe, and you should be suspicious when books do that.

Now, at some point, we do have to look at different parts of the Bible at once to try to see how they fit together. That synthetic (or synthesizing) work of comparison and clarification is important for us theologically. All I am saying is that our first step is to read, and that is a step we often skip. I say this—a thing I've said before in different words—because we are engaged in work of the second step. In this book, we have been skimming the Bible to find instances in which it mentions the angels—the host of heaven—in order to see what we could say about them. That is our purpose, and it is a good thing to do. However, it is also a necessary strategy for a topic like angels since none of the biblical authors cares to discuss angels in any sustained or meaningful way.

Underlying lots of weird ideas about angels (and other theological topics) is usually a fundamental disagreement on how to read the Bible. You may have seen that truth in our discussion of Old Testament texts. The more we import into the Bible what it must have meant or what "they" thought back then, the more we import what we would like the Bible to talk about or say, the more we insist that it conform to our questions, interests, or passions, the more we run the risk of talking when we ought to be listening. I want to reiterate that the first role of the faithful reader of Holy Scripture is simply to listen. On the basis of this careful listening, we begin to more clearly recognize that warp and woof of the God-breathed message of Holy Scripture. Our theology must come from that, and synthetic work of the kind we are doing in this book should not be a distraction from that fundamental task.

This is especially important on a doctrine like angelology because the Bible often does not say as much as we want it to say about angels. That often provokes a desire for more: more knowledge, more insight, more access. That desire often leads to the temptation to speculate without reference to the Bible, to build doctrines based on personal experiences, to receive "facts" uncritically, and so on. We have lots of confusion on angelology because many teachers are uncomfortable saying, "I don't know. Moses doesn't say." Other "teachers" make stuff up because they know people are intrigued and hungry for answers. There is a reason John says, "Test the spirits" (1 John 4:1). Our best test is the knowledge in the Bible.

Well, then, what about the narrative sections of the New Testament? What do they help us learn about angels? Certainly, they do not revise what we already have seen in the Old Testament. Now, they contain a relatively high concentration of activity: they are narrative descriptions and interpretations of the birth, life, death, burial, and resurrection of the Lord Jesus Christ. We are dealing here with a heightened time of spiritual activity. Nevertheless, my discussion of these texts will be brief because we have already been doing the work of observing the motifs.

Matthew

Matthew tells us that an angel came to announce the birth of our Lord to Joseph (Matt. 1:20–21; motif 4).

The angel continues to guide Joseph in a dream in order to protect the young Lord (2:13–23; motif 2). Both of these instances mark out that Jesus is a significant figure, the kind of figure who is presaged by angelic announcement. Recall that because angelic appearances are rare, the presence of an angel is a sign that someone or something important is happening. We actually cheapen the significance of these events when we expect daily life to be chockfull of angels and spiritual visitations.

In Matthew 4, the devil refers to Psalm 91 in an effort to tempt the Lord Jesus. He is tempting him by reminding him that the angels occasionally guard or protect a key figure (motif 2). Because the Messiah is the king of the angels—of the host of heaven—the devil is actually using one of our motifs as his basis for tempting Jesus! However, his temptation does not succeed. Even so, the angels do come and care for him after his temptation (Matt. 4:11). So the fact that Psalm 91 shows the angels protecting a figure who trusts in God is realized in Matthew 4. The same thing happens in Luke's account of the temptation.

In Matthew 13, our Lord offers some insight into the way the angels will be involved in the execution of God's judgment in the future (vv. 39–49). In fact, he reemphasizes the role of the angels in serving God in the last days in Matthew 16:27. These same ideas are repeated in Matthew 24:31–36 as well as Matthew 25:31–41. Hence, there is some emphasis on the future role of angels as God's servants in the day of the Lord. We do not get too many specific details about the last days here, but it is clear that motif 3 is an important image of God's judgment as it has been in the whole Bible.

In Matthew 18:10, we get the only text that could be relevant to the question of guardian angels. In fact, the notion of guardian angels is not biblical—even though it is an early and often attested idea in early Christian nonbiblical writers. The main reason for that is the surrounding religions and religious ideas of the first century had positive and sometimes elaborate and expansive angelologies. This is true of both Jewish and Greek religious ideas. Actually, the interpenetration of Greek and Jewish ideas in the late years BC and early years AD has often been overlooked in popular writings for Christians. Since the idea of guardian angels was already a familiar and somewhat filled-out notion, it would have been easier to think Matthew 18:10 was somehow confirmation that there really were such creatures. That explains why early Christian commentators made such a big deal about guardian angels, even though this verse does not support those viewpoints.

Keep in mind that motif 2 (angels protect or guide a key figure in a Bible story) is also doing some heavy lifting here for people. After all, don't angels sometimes serve as guardians or protectors? Yes, they do. The problem is that motif 2 shows us that God sends angels at specific times to protect or guide specific people. None of the texts we have read about angels suggests that each person has a perpetual guardian who is specifically assigned to him or her from birth or baptism or any other time. I'll speak about this some more in chapter 9. For now, let me say that a Christian has the Holy Spirit of God. You are secure in Christ because of God's promises, not because an unseen creature follows you around.

In Matthew 22:30, Jesus uses information about the angels in his riposte to the Sadducees' doubting of the resurrection. Matthew tells us the Sadducees do not believe in the resurrection. Apparently, part of the reason is because they find that the resurrection would lead to absurd situations—such as a woman being married to a man and all his brothers according to the law. Of course, Jesus's response to them reveals that they do not understand the nature of the resurrection or the nature of the life to come, nor do they understand the nature of the law. He illustrates this ignorance by saying that in the resurrection we (humans) will not marry one another or be given to one another in marriage any longer. Instead, we will be like the angels of heaven. This means we will be like angels with respect to marriage. Angels do not marry or give in marriage because they cannot reproduce. They do not have families. They are not tasked as Adam was to be

fruitful and multiply. The life to come does not contain death or widows or the need for Levirate marriage. There is no threat of losing one's inheritance there. The future world will in many ways be unlike this current one, but the Sadducees can only imagine resurrection to be basically the same life and world we have now. That is their error. So, while Jesus does mention the angels as a way to illustrate the Sadducees' spiritual ignorance, we do not learn anything new about them here. We already knew that they were spiritual creatures, that they have no bodies, and that—therefore—they were not male and female. We already knew that they are not given in marriage.

The final instance of angels in Matthew comes in another announcement (motif 5). This is, of course, the announcement that Jesus has risen from the dead. The women are told by an angel of the Lord to go and make known the good news that Jesus is alive. This message is so surprising and unusual coming as it does from an angel that Jesus himself confirms it for them (Matt. 28:9–10).

Mark and Luke

In Mark and in Luke we find, for the most part, mentions of angels in the same ways as found in Matthew. In fact, in many cases, the authors mention the angels when giving their accounts of the same events in Matthew. For example, Mark notes that the angels minister to Jesus after his temptation (1:13), that the angels will be present at the judgment (8:38; 13:27–32), and that the resurrected will be like the angels in heaven as it pertains to marriage (12:25). Luke mentions some of the same things as Matthew as well: the temptation (4:10), the role of angels in the judgment (9:26; 12:8–9), the message of the angels at Jesus's tomb (Luke 24:2, 23). However, Luke also mentions angels in some places that are unique to his account.

For example, Luke begins his book with the story of an angel—Gabriel—announcing the birth of John the Baptist (1:11–19). This is the same Gabriel we met in the book of Daniel. Likewise, Gabriel speaks to Mary to announce the impending birth of her Son (1:26–38). These are both examples of motif 4. The angels also visit the shepherds of the fields near the birthplace of Jesus to announce the message of the birth of the Savior (Luke 2:9–15). We can see in these examples how significant Jesus's birth was: it was announced in advance to John's parents, to each of Jesus's human parents, and to bystanders at the time of his birth! Jesus is named at his circumcision according to the word the angel had given his parents (v. 21).

Another example of something unique to Luke is the statement that the angels of God have joy over the repentance of a sinner (15:10). This point is made to reiterate what Jesus had already stated in the chapter (15:7): "I tell you, in the same way, there will be more joy in heaven over one sinner who repents than over ninety-nine righteous people who don't need repentance." In fact, this is the large point of the chapter as we can see in the concluding parable as well (15:32)—repentance should be a source of great joy for those who see it. Hence, the angels are an example of a larger point here—not the main idea of the passage. They long to look into the things God is doing, as we saw in Exodus 28 and will see again shortly in John.

Something similar is true for the parable of Luke 16. Jesus tells the story of a poor man who died and, as he puts it, was carried by the angels to Abraham's side. This is consistent with the notion that angels are involved in the execution of God's judgment (motif 3), for his judgment also has a positive side (motif 2). But since he mentions this in passing in his story, it is not possible to conclude whether angels regularly perform such a role.

John

John organizes his account differently from the other three, so some of his material is unique. Regarding our topic, we see only three significant references to angels. The first of these comes in chapter 1:51: "Then he said, 'Truly I tell you, you will see heaven opened and the angels of God ascending and descending on the Son of

Man,'" which is a reference to Genesis 28. The angels are not doing anything in this passage. Instead, Jesus is telling Nathanael that he will see amazing things as well as highlighting that Nathanael's confession (1:49) is more significant than Nathanael realizes. After all, the promise that came to Abraham and continued through Jacob is realized in this Man, Jesus. The angels want to see what is going on—all of God's creation is caught up in the work of this Man.

In John 12, a voice is heard from heaven, but the crowd is not able to identify its source. Some of the people believe it is the voice of an angel, presumably because it sounded to them like thunder. This does not tell us anything in particular about angels. Instead, it tells us what some of the people in that crowd believed. The people do not understand what they are hearing even though the voice comes for their benefit (v. 30).

Finally, John also contains a description of the angels that appeared at Jesus's tomb to announce his resurrection (v. 12).

These details in John do not enlarge the biblical motifs we have seen already, but they do highlight the way angels are often incidental to the story. The angels adorn the picture. They invite us to "look!" to "behold!" something important.

Acts

In Acts, angels appear as actors in the story several times. In Acts 5, an angel rescues the apostles from prison (motif 2), an angel guides Philip in his evangelism (Acts 8:26; motif 2), an angel instructs Cornelius about how to find Peter (Acts 10:3; motif 2), again an angel rescues Peter from prison (Acts 12:7–11; motif 2), an angel kills Herod for acting as if he were God (motif 3), and an angel speaks to Paul in a dream (Acts 27:23; motif 5). There are also some mentions of angels that reflect what characters in the story thought about angels, such as Acts 6:15; Acts 12:15; and Acts 23:8–9; but those episodes do not tell us what is true about angels, just what those people happened to think.

There is also a longer passage mentioning the angels in Stephen's speech in Acts 7. When he gets to the story of Moses after he fled from Egypt, he explains that "an angel appeared to him in the wilderness of Mount Sinai, in the flame of a burning bush" (v. 30). Stephen explains that it was "through the angel who appeared to him in the bush" that God had sent Moses to be a ruler and redeemer of Israel (v. 35). He also mentions that an angel spoke to him and transmitted the law (vv. 38, 53). Stephen's explanation helps us realize that the angel of the Lord is not God, and it shows the mediation of God's messages to his prophet Moses. Stephen is reminding the scribes about their own history in an effort to show that they have always been a stiff-necked and resistant people. The religious leaders do not contest his account or dispute him. They throw rocks at him until he is dead. What stronger evidence of their hard-heartedness could there be?

In all of the narrative texts at the beginning of the New Testament, angels make some appearances either as characters or as figures referred to by characters in the texts. In either case, we do not find an expansion of what they are or what they do but rather further instances of the motifs that were well established in the books written by Moses. I am not saying that there is nothing fresh or important about angels in these later books of the Bible. The angels still adorn the stories in key moments, and their presence helps us realize the significance of the messages they bring or the person they protect. The fact that they are always doing the same things testifies to the consistency of God's message and action.

CHAPTER 7

ANGELS IN THE NEW TESTAMENT LETTERS

W hat we have seen before continues, but there are some subtle differences. The motifs are less frequent in these writings because they are not narratives. We do not find angels doing anything in the letters (Revelation is an exception). Instead, they are mentioned in order to emphasize something else important to the writer. The New Testament letters testify to the reality of angels and, most often, to the threat of misunderstanding them and their place in God's world. Strong emphasis on angels is only found in instances in which referring to angels is used to clarify something for the reader or when the author is describing the day of the Lord.

Paul

Angels do not play a major role in Paul's letters. That does not mean he never mentions angels or that he does not believe in angels. Rather he mentions them in order to support something else he is saying. For example, *angelos* only appears in Romans when Paul is explaining the security a Christian has in the Lord: "For I am persuaded that neither death nor life, nor angels nor rulers, nor things present nor things to come, nor powers, nor height nor depth, nor any other created thing will be able to separate us from the love of God that is in Christ Jesus our Lord" (8:38–39).

The word occurs more frequently in 1 and 2 Corinthians but still in incidental ways. Paul says, "For I think God has displayed us, the apostles, in last place, like men condemned to die: We have become a spectacle to the world, both to angels and to people" (1 Cor. 4:9). Here angels are only mentioned as a way to emphasize that all of creation can behold the spectacle.

Likewise, in 1 Corinthians 6:3, Paul asks a surprising question: "Don't you know that we will judge angels?" This comment is a way for him to intensify what he had already asked in verse 2: "Don't you know that the saints will judge the world?" The point is that the disputes that are dividing them (6:1) should not be beyond their capacity to handle since they are destined from a much wider scope of judgment in the end times. Paul again mentions angels as a point of emphasis.

In 1 Corinthians 11:10, Paul says, "This is why a woman should have a symbol of authority on her head, because of the angels." The idea here is that there is a proper order between a husband and wife, which reflects what they are as a man and woman. The reason this order is important is because the marriage is or should be illustrative of the message of the gospel. Among the brethren, we ought to conduct ourselves in such a way that we showcase our belief in God, his order, his plan, his creation, and so on. Part of that plan and order in God's creation is recognizing the honor due to both men and women and acting in accordance with it. The example Paul has in mind here is how men and women dress, how they cover their heads. Because all creation is caught up in the work of God in Christ, it matters for all creation (including the angels) how men and women conduct themselves in public worship. Paul often refers to angels when he wants us to consider the wider ramifications of what he is teaching us.

This technique continues in 1 Corinthians 13:1 when Paul writes, "If I speak human or angelic tongues but do not have love, I am a noisy gong or clanging cymbal." The point here is not that a man can actually speak the angel's language or that angels even have a language of their own. The point is that absent love no power of any kind no matter how prodigious is worth anything. Hence, he goes on to laud love and mutual edification as the marks of the Spirit's presence and the purpose of the Spirit's gifting of the church.

In 2 Corinthians, Paul refers to the fact that evildoers can present themselves as righteous. Even the emblem of evil—the devil—disguises himself as an angel of light. Paul says "of light" (11:14) to make clear that Satan disguises himself as a good angel, since Satan is (by nature) an angel. I'll discuss this more in chapter 8. Satan appears again in the letter because the "thorn" in Paul's flesh (12:7) is called an *angelos*. Usually, this word is translated as "messenger" and not "angel." Nothing stands or falls on that decision, but it is possible that the word is better understood as angel.

In Galatians 1:8, Paul turns again to referring to angels as a way to make emphasis to his point: "But even if we or an angel from heaven should preach to you a gospel contrary to what we have preached to you, a curse be on him!" He also refers to the angels' participation in bringing the law we discussed from Acts 7. Again, the word *angelos* is used for a point of emphasis when Paul says the Galatians did not scorn or despise him but received him as a messenger from God. In fact, they received him as if he were Christ Jesus himself.

In Colossians, Paul reminds us not to worship angels (Col. 2:18). Because they are part of "everything else," as we have said previously, they are not worthy of our adoration or worship. Yet, in 2 Thessalonians, we are reminded that they will participate in the execution of God's judgment in the last days (1:7). Paul tells Timothy that because Jesus was manifest in the flesh before all creation—even "seen by angels" (1 Tim. 3:16)—we ought to hold fast to that teaching and act accordingly. Hence, he can later charge Timothy to "observe these things" in the presence of all the inhabitants of heaven: God, Jesus, and their host (5:21).

We do not see angels in Paul's writing acting outside the bounds of the motifs established elsewhere in Scripture. Instead, we see Paul referring to their reality as a way to add emphasis or urgency to his message. Because they are real and because God's plan of redemption impacts all creation, he reminds us that how we live and act is a confession not just to flesh and blood but to the whole creation.

Hebrews

Angels are important to the early structure of the book of Hebrews because they enable the writer to highlight that Jesus is greater than they are. He is not only a man; he is the divine Son of God. In chapter 1, the author uses a catena of citations to the Psalms in order to support his proof that Jesus is greater than the angels. Here we will be able to discuss some of the psalms we skipped over in chapter 3. The angels must be lower than Jesus because God speaks to the Son differently from the way he speaks of the angels (Heb. 1:5), because God commands the angels to worship him (1:6), because the angels are creaturely while the Son is an eternal king (1:7–13).

Angels are not divine. They are "ministering spirits sent out to serve those who are going to inherit salvation" (1:14; motif 5). The motifs Moses established show all the ways the angels have served God's people. That these angels are creatures and "spirits," the author makes clear with reference to Psalm 104:6. In chapter 2, he shows the rank of men and angels in the order of creation with reference to Psalm 8. Recall that there is God and everything else. In everything else, there are spirits (angels and demons), creatures that are both spirit and material body (that's us!), and then squirrels, rutabagas, and rocks. This is known in the history of our religion as the hierarchy of being. The author uses the difference between humans and angels in creation to show that Jesus was really a man (made lower than the angels for a little while and suffering death in Heb. 2:9), but he has taken his rightful place as God beside the Father in his ascension from the grave. Because the Son of God became a man, the author can assert that Jesus helps Abraham's offspring, not the angels (Heb. 2:16). There is no redemption for an angel who sins. Sinning angels are actually demons. These creatures will be mentioned in 2 Peter and Jude, but I will focus on them in chapter 8.

Nevertheless, there are angels who do the will of God and worship him in heaven (12:22; motif 1)—the same kingdom to which we are going. In fact, for all we know, we may encounter angels as Lot did (13:2), but we might never know. This instruction (be hospitable!) is a great example of how the Bible testifies the reality of the host of heaven without encouraging us to seek them out or setting up the expectation that we would know what they are doing. You should not expect to encounter an angel, but you should not cease to believe in them either.

Peter

Peter mentions angels a few times in his letters in a way similar to what we find in those of Paul; angels are a point of emphasis. Angels are real. In fact, they long to look into the story of the gospel and its effects (1 Pet. 1:12), a story that includes a message of Jesus's complete authority over all creation—which includes the spiritual realm and angels (3:22). Here the mentions of angels highlight the supremacy of Christ and his work, especially the clear authority he has over all things. In his second letter, Peter uses wicked angels (demons) as a point of emphasis regarding judgment (2 Pet. 2:4). The judgment of the wicked angels, the flood of Noah's time, and the destruction of Sodom and Gomorrah are all examples that show the seriousness and reliability of divine judgment. This mention of angels is a variation on motif 1—the angels that do not worship God are judged. In fact, whereas arrogant people are willing to speak evil of glorious things, good angels do not slander even the wicked (2:10–11). The goodness of holy angels is used to emphasize the wickedness of evil men, and the surety of the final judgment for angels is used to emphasize the surety of God's judgment in his day. I will move on to Jude here because 1–3 John do not mention angels.

Jude

Jude discusses some similar issues to Peter. In verse 6, he mentions angels who abandoned their first state. This refers to the same event Peter mentions (2 Pet. 2:4). This "fall" of the angels is referred to by Jesus in John 8:44, but it is the only mention of this event in Holy Scripture. Because the comments in the Bible on that question are so limited—and for some people unduly—there are enormous nonbiblical commentary traditions that try to tell the "whole" story. However, not only are those traditions of men contradictory with one another, but none of them are also inspired of God or endorsed by the authors of the Bible.

It is important to distinguish between ideas we can find in various retellings of the Bible and what the Bible actually says. Crucially, the point that Jude (or Peter for that matter) is making when he refers to angels is abundantly clear. God did not spare the angels who rejected him (at some undisclosed point in the remote past). He will not pass over human sin either. As further examples, we have the global flood of Noah's time and the destruction of Sodom and Gomorrah.

I'll talk some more about the "fallen" angels in the chapter on demons (chap. 8). For now, we can note that angels are creatures—part of the "everything else"—and they are subject to God's judgment just like the rest of creation. It is God's judgment and no one else's. Even Michael the archangel would not dispute with the devil over the body of Moses (v. 9). The point is clear: not even angels would act as presumptuously as the wicked, and they are higher and more powerful than any man! At the time of God's choosing, however, Michael will enact God's judgment at his command (Rev. 12:7).

Revelation

The angelic motifs return to the foreground in the Revelation of John because the writing returns to narrative elements. In the early chapters of the book, the word *angel* appears in most English translations in the introduction to the letters to the churches (2:1, 8, 12, 18; 3:1, 7, 14), but it is not at all obvious that the word should be translated "angel." Recall that the Greek word *angelos* means "messenger." There are several good reasons for thinking the "angels" of these churches are simply messengers, not celestial beings. First, there is no description of the "angels" that would allow us to conclude with confidence that they are celestial and not human. Second, it would be unprecedented in Holy Scripture if a prophet were to write to a celestial being. Third, it is not at all clear what an angel of a church is, whereas we have many accounts of messengers to churches in the New Testament. Even if the word should be translated "angel," we could at most conclude that these seven churches were somehow in some undisclosed way associated with a particular angel. Apparently, John would have to know enough about that to obey the instructions—in fact, he would have to know how to write a letter to an angel!—but that would not leave us able to know such things or what to make of them. Since there are no patterns in the Holy Scripture that allow us to make sense of the translation "angel" here, the default meaning "messenger" is a clearer and better choice.

In the remainder of the book, by contrast, we see instances of the word *angelos* that clearly refer to spiritual beings, angels. We also see cherubim—creatures that to this point only made lengthy appearances in Ezekiel. Because this section of the book describes John's visions, the angels function to interpret the vision for John, often by introducing major parts of the visions (motif 5). Their activities in the visions are usually associated with judgment because John's vision is of the end times (motif 3). For example, the first angelic creatures John sees are cherubim, worshipping God around his throne (Ezek. 4:6–9; motif 1). The creatures serve the purpose of highlighting the divine figure on the throne and drawing attention to his supremacy and his message. This is the same pattern we saw in Ezekiel.

Next, an angel cries out, "Who is worthy to open the scroll and break its seals?" (5:2; motif 5). This angel's question focuses our attention on the supremacy of the one on the throne who can open the scroll. Again, the angels worship God with their voices (5:12). In chapter 6, the living creatures instruct John to observe the vision of the seals (6:1, 3, 5, 7; motif 5). In chapter 7, John sees a vision in which some angels are prevented from executing God's judgment (motif 3). Again, they worship God in heaven (7:11–12).

In chapters 8–10, John's vision includes angels blowing trumpets to introduce major features of the vision. Angels are functioning here in the same way we saw in the prophets, especially in Zechariah (motifs 3 and 5). In chapter 12, John describes a war in heaven in which Michael and his angels defeat a dragon and his angels. The dragon, whom John calls Satan, is cast out of heaven with his angels (motif 3). In chapter 14, angels bring another message in John's vision (motif 5) as well as execute judgment—a judgment that continues in the vision of chapters 15–16 (motif 3).

In chapter 17, John is visited by another angel who explains the visions to him (vv. 1–3, 7–18). This follows the pattern of motif 5 that we observed in Daniel. Likewise, the messages of the angels in chapters 18, 19, 20, and 21. All of these scenes involve angels punctuating the visions to highlight key images and moments and to offer a sense of their significance to the prophet. Because these are visions of the end, the angels are often depicted in postures of judgment.

I do not rehearse all these chapters in one sentence to make light of the vision John sees. Instead, because this is a book on angels, I am trying to focus our attention on the motifs instead of too quickly being submerged in the particular details of these passages. The function of the angels in these passages is clear, and their actions in executing God's judgment await his timing in a quickly coming future. All the technicolor, spiritual oomph our world may seem to lack will be swift and terrible in the day of the Lord. The same angels that are behind the scenes today will be front and center in the worship of God and in their ministering to his people.

CHAPTER 8

DEMONOLOGY

Some of the angels sinned at the beginning of creation, and they became altogether wicked and evil. The word for those angels is "demons." Some theologians have also called them "fallen angels." *Fallen angels* is not a biblical term, but it helps emphasize that demons are just morally corrupt angels. They are spiritual creatures, moral and rational agents, except that they have become totally corrupted by their first sin. Unlike humans, there is no redemption or repentance for demons. *Fallen* does not mean "fallen from heaven" here: it means a moral or spiritual fall.

I was at a movie recently with a colleague, and there was a preview for a new exorcist film. The preview was supposed to be creepy and weird: some kids disappear for a few days in the forest, and when they return from being lost, they talk and move in weird, uncanny ways. Eventually, they have horrible rasping voices and inverted irises and random bruises and cuts on their faces. I imagine a priest is brought in to do something. If the film is anything like the first one, then there will be lots of grotesque yelling and candles and so on. Aside from lame jump scares, such films are scary on the premise that the audience can be made to buy in: buy in to the belief that maybe there really are demons like that and maybe there is possession like that and, well . . . maybe? Because we have a surprising and often terrifying world, when something unusual happens, the man in the clerical collar can be made to look the hero. After all, he has a special book and usually has command of some Latin phrases.

I'll admit to you something morbid here: I usually find such movies somewhat comical. Not the gore and the screaming and so on, which is gross and upsetting. What I find comical is the complete lack of resonance such films have with the biblical picture of demons. Ostensibly, these sorts of stories—the really creepy ones—are based on some true event. But why is it that exorcisms in the movies are strung out horrific affairs when in Holy Scripture they pass by in a handful of words? Why are medieval Latin remedies especially effective when Latin is not a biblical language? Most of these films depict quasi-magic rituals in which pentagrams have merely been replaced with crosses.

The "demons" in them are not like real demons at all—at least, they are not like the demons as the inspired authors of Holy Scripture talk about them.

Demonology is a place where the temptation to take our scripts from popular media or other religions or anywhere but the Bible is especially strong. I do not know why that is exactly. I imagine it is because we are afraid of things we cannot control and having more detailed stories about creatures like demons gives us a sense of command. After all, the creepiness in exorcist movies is also that the corrupted innocent is totally out of control. People begin to wonder, I imagine, if anything or anyone has command over these evil things. Can they be stopped? Can their malice be ended?

The answer is yes. Whatever they really are or aren't like, however many of them there are, however preternatural your horror after hearing weird cinema tales about them, demons are just creatures God made. He is as in control of them as he is in control of lions, tigers, and bears. And they are no more worthy of worry than those creatures.

Here is a mistake that crops up sometimes: because we know demons are creatures, we try to understand them (maybe even without realizing it clearly!) on the basis of analogies to other creatures we know better. So we think of them like fierce animals, say. I'm not worried about bears because I have a house with walls. Bears can't come in.

But I might worry that I do not have a similar wall for demons. And some charlatan teacher or "exorcist" may come offering just such a wall: some kind of oil or blessing or whatever. All that stuff amounts to nothing more than magic, and real magic—not the lame crystals for sale in your comic bookstore but real magic—Pharoah's kind—is expressly forbidden for God's people. You cannot make yourself more secure from demonic threats by disobeying God. The Bible does not see the schemes of the devil and his demons and offer its own "magical" defense complete with runes and pseudo-Latin words and censers filled with certain herbs that only bloom in twilight. We have a supernatural religion, but we do not have a superstitious one.

The defense you have against the world, sin, and the devil is God: your Father in heaven, the blood of Jesus Christ that washes away your sins, and the Holy Spirit who secures you for the day of redemption. There is nothing better, and you do not need anything else. Let's agree not to take our cue on the spirit realm from what movie makers think, what some friend of a friend claims to have experienced, or what the colorful book in the truck stop spindle says. Let's listen to God's Word.

If we look at what the Bible says about the demons, we can be encouraged by two things: it doesn't say much, and it provides the only prescription we need for anything that ails us. To the first point: the Bible says so little about demons that we can rehearse all that we have said about demons in just one short chapter. Books on demons of any substantial length tend to major on two things: (1) other religions or nonbiblical religious texts and (2) anecdotes. Since this is a book on what the Scriptures say about angels and demons, we can be more concise.

But I can't resist a general anecdote. After all, I'm running a real risk here. When I say, "No, not really," about demons, some people will be tempted to think I do not take them seriously. Some people will be tempted to think I have not had the right kind of experience with these issues, for surely if I had, I would be more open to the "truths" about demons. I have spoken to at least a dozen people who either believed themselves to be "possessed" by demons or were brought to me because other people thought they were possessed. Not one of those people had an evil spirit. They did believe false things about God and the gospel. That stuff is what Paul calls "the teachings of demons" (1 Tim. 4:1). Let me tell you from both experience and the plain reading of Holy Scripture that demons are not something you need to spend time worrying about. That should be your takeaway from this chapter. You need to believe that Satan and his angels are real, that they are set against God's plans and purposes, and that Jesus Christ is your armor against them. That is all.

The real warfare here is to trust in God's promises in the Scripture and not be buffeted about by every new story we hear about the demonic. Fighting sin is what you should be about, not fighting demons. Yet demons are real, and they are really set against us. The Bible says as much, and we need to know what it says.

The Word *Demon*

"Demon" in English comes to us from the Greek word *daimon*. You might find this surprising, but there is no Hebrew word for *demon*. Neither is there any story in the Old Testament about the creation of demons or the fall of angels or any other such thing. Demons don't come up much in Old Testament teaching because the prophets do not care much about them. The reason it is often a big source of reflection and teaching in nonbiblical books in the Greek and Jewish traditions is because demons and intermediaries and spiritual beings are a big deal to those religions and cultures. But they are not a big deal in the Bible. Hence, these other traditions try to fill in the "gaps" with their own ideas. You may have heard people talk about how demons are a big deal, but that is almost always because they have read other religious and cultural ideas into the otherwise clear and concise text of Holy Scripture.

Demons in the Old Testament

Of course, there are some passages of the Old Testament that deal with demons, but we need to use an important distinction when we look for information on demons in the Bible. We have to continue to distinguish between what the text affirms and what the text merely reports. For example, at times, the prophets report that some character believes or worships a "god" or "gods." In 1 Kings 20:23, the advisors to the king of Aram argue that the "gods" of Israel are "gods of the hill country." They are convinced that the Lord is a regional god who only has authority in the hills or mountains. This shows their theology on display. They think of gods as more or less regional powers. But that is not the theology of the author of 1 Kings. Look what the Lord says to the king of Israel through a prophet: "Because the Arameans have said, 'The LORD is a god of the mountains and not a god of the valleys,' I will hand over all this whole huge army to you. Then you will know that I am the LORD" (1 Kings 20:28). The prophets do not believe in other gods besides the Lord, but the pagan peoples of the nation certainly do.

Someone could misunderstand some passages in the Old Testament and believe they affirm the existence of other gods when really they just affirm that those people believe in such gods. The "gods" of the nations are simply vain figments of their own idolatrous hearts. As Psalm 96:5

says, "For all the gods of the peoples are worthless idols, but the LORD made the heavens."

Nevertheless, there are powerful and evil spiritual creatures that masquerade as gods, even though they are not gods. Sometimes the object of worship for an idolator was in fact a demon. Paul explains that food offered to idols is offered to something worthless (as we know from Ps. 96:5), but that does not necessarily mean there is not a spiritual reality behind the worship. He writes in 1 Corinthians 10:19–20: "What am I saying then? That food sacrificed to idols is anything, or that an idol is anything? No, but I do say that what they sacrifice, they sacrifice to demons and not to God. I do not want you to be participants with demons!"

So the "gods" of the nations are either nothing at all, or perhaps they are some formidable spiritual entity: a demon but not a "god."

In the Old Testament, this area is tricky because the main Hebrew word here is *elohim*. It is a word we have seen before. You will remember that it is a word that refers to something spiritual with some degree of power. Sometimes the word is used for the one, true God: "In the beginning, God (*elohim*) made the heavens and the earth" (Gen. 1:1). It is also used to refer to the fictitious gods of the nations (Ps. 96:5) and to refer to human judges or prophets. Speaking to Moses, God says, "He [Aaron] will speak to the people for you. He will serve as a mouth for you, and you will serve as God to him" (Exod. 4:16). Perhaps even clearer, in Exodus 21:6, "His master is to bring him to the judges [*Elohim*]." In fact, the word can just be used to mean "big" or "significant" without relating to spiritual matters at all. In Jonah 3:3, we read: "Now Nineveh was an extremely great city, a three-day walk." The Hebrew that is translated here "extremely great" contains a version of *elohim*. Because the word is ambiguous on its own, we have to be careful about making too many big claims on the basis of the presence of this single word.

Usually, translations of Old Testament texts that use *demon* are based on later teaching in the New Testament. This is because the words used to refer to demons are often ambiguous or—please note this—the words are rare. They do not occur often. For example, the word *saiyr* in Hebrew means "goat." This word is sometimes translated as "demon" in English in two texts: Leviticus 17:7 and 2 Chronicles 11:15. The reason the word is so translated is because some pagan peoples worshiped idols that looked like goats. Notice the context in Leviticus 17:7: "They must no longer offer their sacrifices to the goat-demons that they have prostituted themselves with." Because the text mentions sacrifice and prostitution is a common prophetic metaphor for false worship, the implication is that the "goats" are idols of some sort. Note, however, that the word *idol* does not appear in this text, and, again, there is no Hebrew word for demon. The word is simply "goat." The verse gets translated as "goat-demon" because the notion is that these "goats" are idols of some kind, and we know from Paul that idols are sometimes demons. Goat-idols would be less interpretive.

Hence, the idea is that these nonreal gods (or possibly real demons) were goatlike figures in the minds of the people who worshipped them. That is one of the reasons historically for the cartoon appearance of Satan with horns and goat feet. It is not because there is any depiction of him like that in Holy Scripture. In fact, there are not any depictions of him at all! It is because the image of goat or satyr was associated with false worship that Moses condemned. In the same way artists in the Renaissance used a contemporary image from false religion (Cupid the messenger) as a shorthand way to paint images of celestial messengers, so artists have used the false religious images of pagan religions (goat-demons) to depict the actual ruler of the demons (Satan). But, as interesting as these artistic developments are, we cannot confuse them with what the Bible actually says.

Similarly, in 2 Chronicles 11:15, we read that Jeroboam—a bad guy and idolator—"appointed his own priests for the high places, the goat-demons [*saiyr*], and the golden calves he had made." Again the author is talking about idols. Demons are the spiritual beings that might be receiving the worship of the idol. In any case, neither of these two texts teaches us any details about demons. At most, they show that part of the spiritual realm contains creatures who are opposed to God and love false worship. We call those things "demons." They are real, and they are bad.

The other Hebrew word sometimes translated as "demon" is *shed*. It occurs only in Deuteronomy 32:17 and Psalm 106:37. You will notice in most English translations that the word is translated variously as "demon" or "false god." The reason for that is because any "real" false god is a demon. Still, these Hebrew words do not mean "demon" although they may refer to demons in the English sense of the word. Again, what we learn here is that there are such things as evil spiritual beings.

Likewise, the word for "demon" in Greek (*daimon*) does not always mean demon in the fallen angel sense. Outside of biblical usage especially, the word is much closer in usage to *elohim*: it refers to a formidable spiritual entity of some kind. In the New Testament, however, the word is used to refer to wicked spirits. There are other terms that are also used to refer to the same creatures in the New Testament: unclean spirits (Mark 6:7), evil spirits (Luke 7:21), deceiving spirits (1 Tim. 4:1), or simply angels (Matt. 25:41). In the New Testament a fuller depiction of demonology appears because the biblical authors refer to demons in order to show us something wonderful about Jesus.

Demons in the New Testament

The period of human history disclosed in the Gospel accounts and in the book of Acts is a heightened time of spiritual activity. The Son of God has taken on a human nature. He is born, lives, dies, is buried, and rises on the third day in fulfillment of the Scriptures. He ascends to heaven and pours out the Holy Spirit on his people. One of the ways the Gospel writers emphasize the deity of Jesus is by showing the authority he has over spiritual beings. We have already seen some examples of this with angels. They minister to him after his temptations, for example. They bring messages about him, and they praise him. The Gospel writers also use demons in the same way. When Jesus confronts a demon, he is victorious. Demons fear him. In fact, John says, "The Son of God was revealed for this purpose: to destroy the devil's works" (1 John 3:8). But what are the devil's works? They are not chiefly spooky horror movie stuff: hauntings, possessions, bad dreams, thought-stealing, secret cults, and so on.

In the context, John is referring chiefly to sin. The devil is the "god of this age" (2 Cor. 4:4), the ruler of the demons (Mark 3:22). When John wants to talk about things that oppose Christian living and witness, he names three things: the world, sin, and the devil. These are not three unrelated causes of difficulty in Christian life, as if we should go through a diagnostic to determine exactly which of them is the source of a particular problem. Rather, those three words are shorthand for the whole system Christ has overcome in his substitutionary death for us. In the Gospel accounts, Jesus's defeat and casting out of demons is a way to show he has authority over his enemies. It is a way of showing that he and his message can rescue and heal his people.

Here is another example from James. When speaking of the wisdom appropriate to Christians, he says:

> Who among you is wise and understanding? By his good conduct he should show that his works are done in the gentleness that comes from wisdom. But if you have bitter envy and selfish ambition in your heart, don't boast and deny the truth. Such wisdom does not come down from above but is earthly, unspiritual, demonic. For where there is envy and selfish ambition, there is disorder and every evil practice. But the wisdom from above is first pure, then peace-loving, gentle, compliant, full

of mercy and good fruits, unwavering, without pretense. And the fruit of righteousness is sown in peace by those who cultivate peace. (3:13–18)

Focus on verse 15: "Such wisdom does not come from above but is earthly, unspiritual, demonic." James uses the word *demonic* in parallel with something unspiritual and something worldly or earthly. The inspired writers of the New Testament are not always interested in carefully distinguishing between acute instances of demonic activity over against the generally fallen state of the world. That does not mean "demon" or "demonic" are merely metaphors for the dilapidated spiritual condition of our world. Demons are real, actual spiritual beings. They are as real as lions, tigers, and bears. They are as real as thieves and arsonists and murderers. But they are not the unique, hidden source of trouble in the world. The popular horror film account of demons is not biblical. It oversells how often we would expect individual people to be assaulted by demons, and it undersells how pervasive the effect of earthly, unspiritual, demonic wisdom is in the cultures, false religions, institutions, and human behavior of our world.

Yet demonic attacks do happen. Just what is happening with people and demons in the New Testament narratives? The word the Bible writers use to describe a person who is being affected by demons is "demonized." Some older English translations translate the Greek word as "possessed," but the word does not really mean possessed. Then why do they translate it that way? Early English translations often used the Latin version for some words because of its long history of use in the Christian churches. The Latin versions of the Bible translate the Greek word *daimonizomai* as *possideo*, which is the Latin word for "possessed." *Possessed* is therefore a better translation of the Latin word than it is a translation of the Greek word. After all, we can see from the usage in the New Testament that people who are afflicted or affected by a demon are not always possessed, which suggests that they are totally under the control of a demon. Rather, the "demonized" range in intensity and effect. We can look at the examples in the Gospel accounts fairly quickly because there are not that many of them. They are intended to be representative, and, crucially, they are solely meant to emphasize the divine authority of the Son of God. They are not narrative manuals on how to combat demons. Let's see what they say.

Matthew

The first instance of demonic activity in Matthew's Gospel is found in chapter 4 in which the devil tempts Jesus in the wilderness. The purpose of this narrative is to show that Jesus is greater than the devil but also that he is greater than Adam. Unlike Adam, he does not succumb to temptation of the devil even though he is hungry (4:2) and in the wilderness (4:1). Contrast that to Adam in a plentiful garden whose name means "luxury." The story helps establish Jesus as the only one who can do the will of the Father, which is an important theme for Matthew's account.

Later in chapter 4, Matthew offers a summary statement of Jesus's ministry. He tells us that Jesus was teaching and healing in the synagogues. What follows in the book is a major summary of his teaching and key examples of his healings. Verse 24 mentions that the people brought to him the "demon-possessed" as well as those who had other diseases, including "epileptics, and the paralytics." The people had no trouble distinguishing between an instance of demonic activity and a "natural" sickness or illness.

In the following sections of the book, the power Jesus has over demons is repeatedly emphasized. In chapter 8, we have another general account: "When evening came, they brought him many who were demon-possessed. He drove out the spirits with a word" (8:16). This is followed by some specific examples: the Gadarene demoniacs (8:28–33) and the man struck mute by a demon (9:32). These two events show us that demons affect people in more than one way.

The crucial scene is found in Matthew 12. Jesus heals a demonized man, and—finally it seems to a reader of Matthew—the crowd asks if Jesus is the Son of David (12:23). This is the crucial point because Matthew has started his account by identifying Jesus as that very person (1:1). The Pharisees, however, accuse Jesus of having power over the demons only because he is in league with Beelzebul, the ruler of the demons (12:24). Jesus rebukes them sharply by showing how unreasonable their response is (Why would Satan drive out Satan? [12:26]) and by illuminating the correct response to his power. "If I drive out demons by the Spirit of God, then the kingdom of God has come upon you" (12:28). This is what the conflict between Jesus and the demons he encounters is really intended to show: Jesus's authority and power and the presence of the kingdom.

In contrast to the faithlessness of the Pharisees, the last example of Jesus's interaction with a demonized person is found in chapter 15. In this passage a non-Jewish woman—a Canaanite—cries out to Jesus to heal her demonized daughter. She addresses him as "Son of David"! Jesus responds to her persistent faith by healing her daughter.

Both of these instances illustrate the relationship between the stories of Jesus's healings and what Matthew wants us to understand about demons. Matthew is not inviting us to become exorcists; he is providing more and more evidence that Jesus is the Christ.

The last example of demonic activity in the book confirms this insight (17:14–20). A man whose son is tormented by a demon comes to Jesus for help because Jesus's disciples could not help him. This shows us that there are some things his disciples cannot do. Yet Jesus is able to heal the boy with a rebuke. He is greater than we are, and he is a sufficient defense against the powers of darkness.

Mark

In his own way, Mark narrates some of the same events as Matthew. We find, for example, a summary statement of Jesus's authority over demons (1:32–34, 39). Jesus encounters resistance from the scribes who ascribe his ability to cast out demons to the devil (3:22). Mark tells us about Jesus's healing of the Gadarene demoniac (5:12–18) and the healing of the pagan woman's daughter (7:26–30). These stories reinforce Jesus's authority. Mark likewise emphasizes the difference between Jesus and his disciples. He gives limited authority to his apostles to affect the demons during their ministry. Mark relates that the disciples were concerned that someone they did not know was casting out demons in the name of Jesus (9:38). Jesus does not share their concern (9:39–40).

Luke

Luke's account reinforces the same posture as both Mark and Matthew. Early in the book, Luke establishes Jesus's authority over demons (Luke 4:34–35; 6:18; 7:21). He emphasizes that demons are aware of who Jesus is (4:41). Luke tells again of Jesus's rebuke of the demon Legion (8:26–38). He gives the apostles' authority over demons when he sends them out (9:1), but they do not have the same power that he has (9:37–42). This becomes important in the structure of Luke because the ability to cast out demons is not what Jesus emphasizes for his disciples. When the larger group of disciples returns from the errand Jesus had sent them on to preach the gospel, they are joyous. They tell Jesus, "Even the demons submit to us in your name" (10:17). But Jesus tells them that such spiritual power is not what they should be thankful for. In fact, he says, "Don't rejoice that the spirits submit to you, but rejoice that your names are written in heaven" (10:20). Celebrating authority over demons is celebrating the wrong thing.

Again, as in Matthew and Mark, Luke recounts that some teachers discount Jesus's ability to cast out demons by attributing it to the devil. In Luke's account, Jesus uses the phrase "finger of God" (Luke 11:20) to describe the power he has over demons. This is a phrase Bible readers know from Moses's encounter with the magicians of

Pharoah (Exod. 8:19). Pharoah's magicians warned him that they could not replicate the things Moses was doing because Moses was doing them by God's authority. They had only the authority of their "gods" (Exod. 12:12). The Pharisees were foolishly attributing Jesus's power to the demons when, in fact, the same power had been over-throwing demons since the days of Moses. Likewise, Jesus teaches that casting out a demon is not the real work that needs to be done (Luke 11:24–26); instead what one needs is trust in and obedience to God (11:28, 32). Furthermore, the scribes try to accuse Jesus of wrongdoing because he is willing to exercise his authority on the Sabbath (Luke 13:10–17). It is righteous to resist Satan even on the Sabbath.

John

John deals with the same issue. Numerous times in John's account Jesus is described as having a demon because of what he says or does (John 7:20; 8:48, 52; 10:20). This appears to be a generic slur, a figure of speech designed to discredit Jesus. But the accusation shows the lack of faith and understanding of those who make it. In every case the slur is designed to indicate that Jesus is lying—usually about his relationship to the Father. In John 7:20, the accusation that he has a demon comes after Jesus teaches that he has come to do the Father's will. In chapter 8, the accusations come after Jesus reiterates the same teaching. The same thing happens in chapter 10 (vv. 14–18). However, the fact that Jesus can heal and cast out demons is decisive from some people that Jesus cannot have a demon: "These aren't the words of someone who is demon-possessed. Can a demon open the eyes of the blind?" (10:21).

In all four Gospel accounts, Jesus's authority over the demons is a sign of his authority in general. It is a sign that he is Lord of heaven and earth. The teaching on demons here is incidental. They are merely tools to indicate the centrality, authority, majesty, and dominion of Lord Jesus. In the same way angels are used by New Testament authors to emphasize something crucial about God, so also demons.

Acts

In Acts, the apostles begin to spread the word about Jesus from Jerusalem and Judea, to Samaria, and to the ends of the earth (1:8). Luke emphasizes the presence of the Holy Spirit in this ministry by highlighting instances in which the apostles' ministry is similar to what Jesus had done in the Gospel accounts. For example, in Acts 5, the people from near Jerusalem bring the sick and the demonized to be healed (v. 16). However, this activity is not strongly emphasized throughout Luke's narrative of the gospel's early spread. Luke does, however, use instances of demonic healing at each major part of the book to highlight the presence of God's Spirit. Hence, the healings at Jerusalem (5:16), in Samaria (8:7), and even among the Gentiles (16:18). Yet it is important to notice that the emphasis for Luke is not on the ability of the apostles to cast out demons or to do signs and wonders. Instead, the emphasis is on the preaching of God's Word. Notice in the case of the girl with a spirit that allowed fortune-telling (16:16), Paul does not cast the demon out of her as soon as he can. In fact, he does not "for many days" until he is "greatly annoyed" (16:18). When he does offer the command, the demon leaves immediately. In contrast to the words of Paul, the Jewish exorcists have no authority of evil spirits (19:13–16). This shows that exorcism is not some magic ritual in which saying the correct words at the right time has some automatic effect. Jesus's disciples already knew that words were not enough (Matt. 17:19).

The Rest of the New Testament

In the rest of the New Testament, demons are infrequently mentioned. The word for "demon" occurs only around ten times in the New Testament outside the passages we have discussed. Four occurrences are in the passages of 1 Corinthians we already discussed, in which Paul equates the false gods of the nations with demons.

Likewise, we have read already how he warns of false teaching against the gospel in the days to come, referring to such teaching as "teaching of demons" and attributing such nonsense to "deceitful spirits" (1 Tim. 4:1). Of course, John notes the same things about the end time, equating idols and demons (Rev. 9:20) and warning against false teaching (16:14).

We do not find instructions for dealing with demons aside from prayer and trust in Jesus Christ. In fact, in the most famous "spiritual warfare" passage—a term that came to the fore in our language in the late twentieth century—the commands all have to do with resting in Jesus and praying. There is nothing about magic or rituals or seeking out demons or strongholds. Paul writes:

> Finally, be strengthened by the Lord and by his vast strength. Put on the full armor of God so that you can stand against the schemes of the devil. For our struggle is not against flesh and blood, but against the rulers, against the authorities, against the cosmic powers of this darkness, against evil, spiritual forces in the heavens. For this reason take up the full armor of God, so that you may be able to resist in the evil day, and having prepared everything, to take your stand. Stand, therefore, with

> the truth like a belt around your waist,
> righteousness like armor on your chest,
> and your feet sandaled with readiness for
> the gospel of peace. In every situation take
> up the shield of faith with which you can
> extinguish all the flaming arrows of the
> evil one. Take the helmet of salvation and
> the sword of the Spirit—which is the word
> of God. Pray at all times in the Spirit with
> every prayer and request, and stay alert
> with all perseverance and intercession for
> all the saints. (Eph. 6:10–18)

Paul acknowledges that there are spiritual forces
arrayed against Christ and his people. He insists we keep
in mind that the struggle to cling to Christ and his promises and to live his way in the midst of this world is a real
struggle against forces of darkness arrayed against us. But
the commands he offers us are to put on the armor of God,
to stand, and to pray. Paul uses the notion of "putting on"
often to refer to believing in Jesus Christ (Rom. 13:12–14;
Gal. 3:27; Eph. 4:24; Col. 3:10; 1 Thess. 5:8). When he
talks about armor, he uses images from Isaiah 59. In that
chapter, God does not see anyone to save the people, so
he does it himself. Jesus Christ is the Christian's armor
against the assaults of the enemy. Given the other notions
Paul provides, unbelief and false teaching about the Lord

and his promises are the chief assaults against us. Paul refers to the armor as a defense against the forces arrayed against us because the image ends with this promise in Isaiah: "The Redeemer will come to Zion, and to those in Jacob who turn from transgression" (Isa. 59:20).

Demons are not a major concern for the writers of the Old and New Testaments. This does not mean they do not believe there are demons or that we should be lackadaisical about them. It does mean we should not be worried about them or make them out to be scarier or more horror film-esque than they are. Very little of the total teaching of the Bible is concerned with them. Our concerns and fears should be proportioned accordingly.

Students sometimes ask me, "What if I encounter someone who is demonized? What then?" Then you should pray with and for them, that the Lord of heaven and earth who is able would free them from bondage of the demons and that they would believe in the message of the gospel. That message contains the power of God to salvation (Rom. 1:16). We are not promised the ability to command the demons, but we are promised a refuge in God (Ps. 46:1). Our delight should be in the salvation of our souls, not in our authority over angels and demons.

CHAPTER 9

~~~~~~~

COMMON QUESTIONS
ABOUT ANGELS
AND DEMONS

This chapter is meant to be a rapid-fire series of responses to questions I get quite often about angels and demons. I'll be brief because I'm presupposing the angelic motifs in the Scripture we have already surveyed. In your doctrine, you should be inclined to dismiss teaching on angels and demons unless it participates in the Bible patterns. Always ask yourself whether the viewpoint could be shown from the Bible. Even then, since these matters are not central to the biblical storyline or Christian theology, you do not need to be contentious unless perhaps someone is given a doctrine a pride of place that it should not have. Because there is much speculation masquerading as fact on these issues, the number of potential questions is probably limitless. It is more faithful—easier, even—to look at what Scripture says and cling to that than to respond to all the things it doesn't say.

Do I Have a Guardian Angel?

No. There is a history among Christians of believing in guardian angels, but those traditions are generated from the philosophical and religious milieu of early Christianity theology. No texts of Scripture support the notion that you have a guardian angel. We know from the motifs in Scripture that angels do occasionally protect or guide a major figure, but only in Matthew 18:10 do we have a text that might imply that every Christian was protected by his or her own angel. Matthew 18:10 says, "See to it that you don't despise one of these little ones, because I tell you that in heaven their angels continually view the face of my Father in heaven." The "little ones" refers to the disciples of Jesus, so some people have thought each disciple must have an individual angel in heaven. Couldn't that be right? Doesn't Hebrews 1:14 say that angels are ministering spirits sent to serve those who will inherit salvation? Sure, but none of these passages allows us to infer that every one of us receives a secret angel guardian. What's more, the angels of the little ones are in heaven gazing at the Father. Jesus's point is not to teach or confirm that we all have spirit guides. It is to say that each disciple matters greatly to God, and it is foolhardy to overlook them because of God's love for them. We know that is true because Christ himself says in Matthew's account, "I am with you always" (28:20). You do not need a creature to make you safe if you have the Creator.

Are There Territorial Spirits?

No. There are no texts of Scripture that would allow you to build a doctrine of choirs, hierarchies, regional powers, or any other such topology or organization structure for the spiritual realm. The belief in territorial spirits is pagan. Some writers have tried to say that those pagan beliefs reflect some element of truth and that there are "hints" in Holy Scripture to that effect, but there is no reason to believe them. The main arguments involve speculation about what the biblical authors must have thought given what nonbiblical authors who wrote different books in different languages in a supposedly similar time period wrote in their own religion's books. For example, it is common in some theories to point out that some people in the ancient Near East believed in councils of gods. That fact is supposed to color our understanding of what God's prophets mean when they talk about the host of heaven. But why would it? The prophetic writers of Holy Scripture are not mere men of their times; they are the inspired writers of Holy Scripture. See the discussions of Deuteronomy and Daniel in the earlier chapters for more.

It is true that angels and demons exist in some kind of ranking or order—Michael is an archangel, for example. Satan is said to have his angels. The notion of choirs of angels or elaborate lists of ranks are almost all the fruit of the sixth century. At that time, there was a man who pretended to be the Dionysius mentioned in Acts 17:34. He wrote a series of famous books, one of which was called *The Celestial Hierarchy.* Because people believed he was a near associate with Paul, they gave his writings more credence than they should have. He specifies a series of ranks of angels based on some common words in the New Testament, but a near contemporary of his offers a different list. We should not give unwitting allegiance to a man we do not know who lied about who he was. Even in the rare text that "peels back the curtain" on the spiritual realm, it is not at all obvious that the angels in question are regional lords of territories. Michael, for example, is called the prince of "your people" in Daniel. This means he is the prince of the Jews, who are in exile. They are not even in their own territory! So whatever association exists between Michael and Daniel's people is simply not grounds to hold to a robust view of territorial spirits.

The notion of territorial spirits has been pervasive in some forms of world evangelization. Unfortunately, the information and "research" done on these areas is usually derived from what false religions teach about the spiritual realm. For example, Christians might ask a recent convert from an animistic religion for information on the demons in that region. Not only is this practice never endorsed by Holy Scripture, but it is also actively condemned. Asking a magician or witch doctor for information on the spiritual realm is literally asking for doctrine from demons. We already have the gospel of Jesus Christ. It does not know boundaries or borders or territories. It is the power of God to salvation to all people everywhere.

Do People Become Angels When They Die?

No. The Bible teaches that angels and humans are different kinds of creatures. You do not become an angel when you die for the same reason you do not become an aardvark. You are a different type of creature. The only argument in favor of the view that we become angels when we die is the argument from cartoon death, but we should not take our doctrines from Warner Brothers cartoons (although they are fun to watch).

Are There Possessions Today?

Sure. But the New Testament, as we have seen, does not describe how to perform an exorcism, does not refer to or explain a spiritual gift of exorcism, does not prescribe members of local churches to engage with demons, does not give them that much attention at all. At one point, as we saw, the apostle Paul only performs an exorcism because he is annoyed!

Instead, the remedy we see for demonic presence, false teaching, worldly ideas, sins, betrayal, witchcraft, hypocrisy, theft, adultery, murder, hatred, loathing, self-loathing, sadness, pain, suffering, arson, drunkenness, dissension, and disobedience is the gospel of Jesus Christ.

Christians certainly cannot be demon possessed. There is no biblical evidence that they can be, and it does not fit with biblical evidence. No demon can control a child of God inhabited by the Holy Spirit. You see, possession is not like sickness. In the chapter on demonology, we saw that the Gospel writers distinguished between Jesus's healing those with demons and those with various illnesses. The New Testament indicates that we will struggle with sickness in this life. It does not indicate that we will struggle with possession. There are no tests for demon possession in the New Testament. There is no mention of a gift for exorcism. There are no instructions for exorcism. This is not to say they cannot be engaged in real spiritual conflict. Yet we must remember that we cannot be driven by anecdotes in our theology. Our spiritual beliefs must have their basis in the Bible. Prayer and fasting are the only tools we see commended for spiritual warfare, and those are patterns of Christian living, not signal tools against demons.

We have already seen that *possession* is not really a biblical word. The word is *demonized*. Demonization varies in type and intensity from generating disease-like symptoms to genuine control of the person. In all the accounts of demons in Scripture, not one indicates that believers can be inhabited by demons. There are also no indications that you could "secretly" have a demon. Any argument to the contrary is based on silence—what the Bible does not say—or a claimed personal experience, which should be interpreted from Scripture and not used as a basis for a new type of ministry. There are no acute spiritual conditions for which the Bible provides absolutely no teaching. The Bible claims for itself that it is sufficient for faith and ministry.

In any case, Christians have the Holy Spirit. Notice in our perusal of Holy Scripture how quick the demons were to flee the presence of Christ. There is no room for both the Holy Spirit and a demon in a person. The Bible is clear that demons can fight against believers, but the examples of how they do this are lies about the gospel, clouded doctrines, and false teachers. Take heart that John says, "The one who is born of God keeps him, and the evil one does not touch him" (1 John 5:18).

Is Satan Omnipresent?

No. He is a creature. He is not a "bad" version of God. That is a pagan idea. The key distinction in the Christian worldview and in Christian theology is the distinction between God and everything else. I tell my students that distinction will solve all your problems. Well, all your intellectual problems. (It won't make that special someone notice you!) Satan is part of the everything else. He is one of the things God made. So is every angel. So is every demon. So are humans, rutabagas, and rocks. Satan is evil, and he is powerful; but he does not have divine power, authority, or attributes.

Are Christians Tempted by Satan?

No. I often tease my students, "Unless you rise to the level of Adam or Jesus, you do not need to worry about being tempted by Satan directly." We see his schemes through intermediaries much more often than not. Hence, you can say, "Satan is tempting me," if you are using the word *Satan* as shorthand for all the wrongheaded, ungodly, worldly, demonic, sinful characteristics of our world. But, if you mean "the particular individual called Satan is actively setting himself to tempt me to a particular sin," you are almost certainly wrong. James says that our own sinful natures are enough: "But each person is tempted when he is drawn away and enticed by his own evil desire" (James 1:14). We cannot blame all our problems on Satan.

Yet Paul says that the tempter can tempt people away from the message of the gospel (1 Thess. 3:5). This does not come from evil thoughts he inserts through secret powers. It comes from outward persecutions (2:14). It comes from obstacles to the preaching of the gospel (2:18). After all, John says that "the whole world is under the sway of the evil one" (1 John 5:19). The apostles do not care to distinguish between the world, sin, and the devil because all three are obstacles to our union with God, and they cooperate in manifold ways.

Is Satan a Fallen Angel?

Yes. He is described in the company of angels in Scripture (Matt. 25:41). He was once good but sinned against the Lord (John 8:44). However, the narrative of John 8:44 is the only real account of this transition in the Bible. No account is given in the Bible of his creation or of his moral failing. There are some passages in the major prophets that people sometimes point to for more information, but none of them are about the devil. We do a real disservice to the prophet's message to read them that way.

What Is Going on in Job 1?

Satan is being a real jerk. The book of Job frames the story about Job and his friends by showing a contest of sorts between God and Satan. Among the host of heaven, Satan alone doubts that Job has an authentic trust in the Lord. The rest of the book shows him to be foolish. It also—crucially—shows that he is subservient to God's purposes, for he can only do what God has allowed him. He is a creature. God doesn't run his plans by his creatures or the angels in order to make sure they are okay. He alone is Lord of all things and the Creator of everything.

Do Angels Still Speak to Us Today?

No. I should say, I guess they could speak to us if God wanted them to do so. However, nothing in the Bible sets us to expect that they would. God's final word was given in his Son Jesus (Heb. 1:1–4), and the teachings of his prophets and apostles testify to that fact. Some branches of Christianity do not believe in the doctrine called the sufficiency of Scripture. Hence, members of those sects are primed to believe that God will regularly provide ongoing or updated revelation about his plans and purposes. Of course, this often involves the claim that angels are bringing messages. But every message has to be tested against what is already given to God's people (Gal. 1:8). Most accounts of angelic visitation ignore the patterns of angelic activity in the Bible. Hence, we should be suspicious of such stories.

Who Are the Nephilim?

The Nephilim do not have anything to do with angels or demons. They are mentioned in Genesis 6. They play a big role in some nonbiblical texts, but they do not play a big role in the Bible. Let's look at the context of Genesis 6 to see what it says about them and take our cues from Moses. The relevant bit is the first part of verse 4: "The Nephilim were on the earth both in those days and afterward, when the sons of God came to the daughters of mankind, who bore children to them."

The Nephilim are not the children of the sons of God and daughters of men. The clause in which they are mentioned provides background information about the period in which those marriages took place. This is a common technique the prophets use in their books, and it is a common feature of Hebrew grammar. In nonbiblical retellings of the period before the flood, the Nephilim are described as the offspring of these illicit marriages, but Moses does not say that.

When that period of history is discussed in the New Testament, Jesus describes it by saying, "In those days before the flood they were eating and drinking, marrying and giving in marriage, until the day Noah boarded the ark" (Matt. 24:38). That is all Genesis 6 describes. If the Nephilim were a big deal to understanding that story, surely our Lord would have said something. But he didn't. Neither did any of his prophets or apostles.

Is the Angel of the Lord Jesus?

No. Please don't throw rocks. This is a pretty common misconception. In fact, I would say it is popular. If you have read through the book, you will have noticed that in common passages used to make the theological point that the angel of the Lord is Jesus in disguise I did not say anything much about the matter. The reason is that the angel of the Lord isn't Jesus. I have also said repeatedly that angels are not a big deal compared to Jesus. We must not confuse the angel of the Lord with the Lord. That is an error the characters of Scripture sometimes fall into, and the narrative corrects for their misunderstanding. We have seen that as well (for example, in Judges).

But to make it plain, there are three major reasons the angel of the Lord is not Jesus: grammatical, canonical, and theological. The grammatical one should be enough. Our theology cannot say what the grammar cannot support. I'll start there. It boils down to the suggestive power of "the."

In Hebrew the phrase that gets translated in English as "the angel of the Lord" does not contain the word "the." It is simply the phrase *malak Yahweh*. *Malak*, as we know, is the word for messenger or angel. *Yahweh* is God's name. In phrases like that in Hebrew ("construct phrases"), we translate into English using the definite article "the" whenever the second word in the phrase (in this case *Yahweh*) is a personal name. The added words are because of how English grammar works, not because of what it means in Hebrew. In Hebrew, the definite article (the word *the*) is demonstrative. It means "this one that I am talking about." It does not have a *monadic* function. A *monadic* article is one that means "the one and only." When people read the English phrase, "the angel of the Lord," they sometimes read the word "the" as monadic. They read "the one and only angel of the Lord." That is simply a misunderstanding. Hebrew does not work like that. Two quick examples can show you why.

The first is a similar phrase to *malak Yahweh*: *ebed Yahweh*. *Ebed* means "servant." We would translate that phrase "the servant of the Lord." "The servant of the LORD" is Moses (Deut. 34:5), except for when he is Joshua (Josh. 24:29). The phrase is not a title for only one individual. That is not how those phrases work. So, just as the phrase *ebed Yahweh* does not mean that there is only one figure who is the servant of the Lord, so also the phrase *malak Yahweh* does not mean there is only one figure who is the angel of the Lord.

What's more, take a look at Haggai 1:13. In Hebrew, the verse reads *Haggai malak Yahweh*. That is translated into English as Haggai, the Lord's messenger or the messenger of the Lord. Why? Because *malak* means "messenger," and it is clear that Haggai is not an angel. Yet the prophet can be called *malak Yahweh* because the phrase does not always refer to a single identified individual. It does not always even refer to an angel. The phrase *malak Yahweh* cannot and does not refer to a single identified figure skipping through the pages of the Old Testament because the prophet uses the exact phrase to describe Haggai.

Let me emphasize something important: this is not a problem with the translations. Students sometimes get a bit nervous when I start talking in class about translations and variants and so on. After all, some popular authors have made a big deal out of text criticism and manuscripts in order to undermine the Bible. Here is a secret: all the people who help make your English Bible know all about that stuff. We learn languages, study manuscripts, and learn textual history. We learn about other texts and religions from the same time periods. And we have done that for a long time. We work hard to produce the best work we can to bring you as close to the originals as you can get. So, please, do not hear me saying that your Bible tricked you into thinking the angel of the Lord was Jesus. It has not.

Why? Because it is correct to translate the phrases with the definite article "the." The problem is not with the translations; it is with developing an interpretation that does not understand how the underlying grammatical constructions work. Notice that in the chapters of the book I have shown just from the passages as you have them in English that the angel of the Lord was not the Lord. I did not have to bring up the grammatical argument because you would not need to know all those details to understand the passages. However, I do bring up the grammatical issues here because they slam the door on the wrong reading.

The second reason is canonical. We have already seen that in some famous instances in which "the angel of the Lord" phrase is used, later books of the Bible describe the figure as an angel. This is what happens with Hosea's account of Jacob's wrestling with an angel (Gen. 32; Hosea 12). This is likewise what happens with Stephen's account of Moses's encounter at the burning bush (Exod. 3; Acts 7). Likewise, we saw that the misidentification of the angel with God was often an example of the people's inability to understand God rightly.

The third reason is theological. Jesus is not and was not ever an angel. Jesus is the incarnate Son of God: the eternal second Person of the Godhead who has taken on a human nature (John 1:14). He comes after generations of waiting in the fullness of time (Gal. 4:4). He comes to rescue Abraham's sons, not angels (Heb. 2:16).

The idea that the angel of the Lord is the preincarnate Word of God is popular, but it is based on a misunderstanding of how the Hebrew language works. It is also based on a strong and understandable desire to find Jesus in the Old Testament. After all, for many Christians, the Old Testament can seem odd, foreign, unrelated to us, our daily lives, and Christianity. The solution for that is a better and more careful understanding of the Bible. Jesus is the central concern of the whole Bible. But he "appears" in the passages according to the inspired author's method, interest, timing, and so on based solely on the message and story God is inspiring them to tell. We do not have to help the Old Testament be a Christian book. It is already the majority of our one two-testament Christian Scripture.

Do Angels Sing?

This one hurts a bit. The verb "to sing" is not used with the angels in the Bible. Sometimes translators will render a verb in Job as sing: "The morning stars sang together and all the sons of God shouted for joy" (Job 38:7). However, the Hebrew verb in question—*ranan*—does not mean "sing." It means "make a loud noise." That is why it is used in parallel to "shout" in the verse. We see angels crying out, declaring, shouting, and so on, but not necessarily singing.

EPILOGUE

I've told you that I am a reluctant angelologist because it involves so frequently saying, "No, not really." But there is an aspect of that tendency to say no that I think is vitally important for us. The level of our curiosity about certain matters is not always an indication of the importance of those matters. Angels are a great example. The word *angel* sparks all kinds of questions and flights of imagination. But, if we remember that in fact they are messengers, we will also realize that it is their message that matters most.

In this book, I have tried not to discourage curiosity about the angels so much as I have tried to clarify their place and role in our theology. In doing so, I have offered a view of reading and interpreting the Bible. At the root of many differences of opinion or approaches to the questions of angels is an underlying difference of opinion on the Bible and how to read it. I have tried to say that in reading the text of the Bible—not in imaginative retellings of its stories—we find what the prophets and apostles wanted us to know. I tried to say this because it is what the historic Christian view of the Bible says: the words of the prophets and apostles are inspired of God. My nay-saying (such as it is) is aimed at reminding us of this larger commitment. So, if it feels as though I have taken something away from you (say, that angels don't necessarily sing in choirs), it is only because I think there is something better to replace it.

When we let the angels simply be the messengers they are, we are in a much better position to appreciate the sort of message they bring. More importantly, we can aim our curiosity at the one who commands such messengers.

When the shepherds saw the appearance of an angel of the Lord, Luke says that they feared a great fear. The message of the angel to them was:

> "Don't be afraid, for look, I proclaim to you good news of great joy that will be for all the people. Today in the city of David a Savior was born for you, who is the Messiah, the Lord. This will be the sign for you: You will find a baby wrapped tightly in cloth and lying in a manger."
>
> Suddenly there was a multitude of the heavenly host with the angel, praising God and saying: Glory to God in the highest heaven, and peace on earth to people he favors! (Luke 2:10–14)

Luke goes on to say that, after the angels had left them for heaven, the shepherds took their message to heart. "Let's go straight to Bethlehem and see what has happened, which the Lord has made known to us" (Luke 2:15).

The point of this story is not to teach us how to respond to the angels, but it does help us focus our attention on what really matters. It is not that the angels appeared—that's theme music—but the one to whom they gave testimony—the Messiah, the Lord. He is the star of the show. The shepherds know this. They go to see what "the Lord has made known to us" through them.

The Lord has not disguised from us what he wants us to know. He has made plain to us in writing in the Bible, even the gospel, which the angels long to look into (1 Pet. 1:12). I hope I have shared in this book how angelology teaches us to redirect our gaze not merely from the earthly to a hidden, spiritual realm. That would only redirect our attention to another thing God made, another part of his creation. Instead, we must redirect our gaze all the way up to the Lord, who created heaven and earth, who alone does as he pleases with angels and with men (Dan. 4:35). Holy Spirit, make it so. Amen.

The Word *Angel* in Holy Scripture

I have placed here a list of the verses in which the word *malak* or *angelos* occurs with the meaning "angel." You may have a few differences in your Bible because your translators may have made some different decisions than those I argued for in this book. That's okay: those differences will not undermine any of the motifs I showed you in the earlier chapters, nor will they change the shape of the angelology I have tried to persuade you to hold. Of course, as I noted, some other words can be used to mean angel or to refer to angelic beings, but these are the most relevant texts.

Genesis 16:7: The angel of the LORD found her by a spring of water in the wilderness, the spring on the way to Shur.

Genesis 16:9: The angel of the LORD said to her, "Go back to your mistress and submit to her authority."

Genesis 16:10: The angel of the LORD said to her, "I will greatly multiply your offspring, and they will be too many to count."

Genesis 16:11: The angel of the LORD said to her, "You have conceived and will have a son. You will name him Ishmael, for the LORD has heard your cry of affliction."

Genesis 19:1: The two angels entered Sodom in the evening as Lot was sitting in Sodom's gateway. When Lot saw them, he got up to meet them. He bowed with his face to the ground.

Genesis 19:15: At daybreak the angels urged Lot on: "Get up! Take your wife and your two daughters who are here, or you will be swept away in the punishment of the city."

Genesis 21:17: God heard the boy crying, and the angel of God called to Hagar from heaven and said to her, "What's wrong, Hagar? Don't be afraid, for God has heard the boy crying from the place where he is."

Genesis 22:11: But the angel of the LORD called to him from heaven and said, "Abraham, Abraham!" He replied, "Here I am."

Genesis 22:15: Then the angel of the Lord called to Abraham a second time from heaven.

Genesis 24:7: The Lord, the God of heaven, who took me from my father's house and from my native land, who spoke to me and swore to me, "I will give this land to your offspring"—he will send his angel before you, and you can take a wife for my son from there.

Genesis 24:40: He said to me, "The Lord before whom I have walked will send his angel with you and make your journey a success, and you shall take a wife for my son from my clan and from my father's family."

Genesis 28:12: And he dreamed: A stairway was set on the ground with its top reaching the sky, and God's angels were going up and down on it.

Genesis 31:11: In that dream the angel of God said to me, "Jacob!" and I said, "Here I am."

Genesis 32:1: Jacob went on his way, and God's angels met him.

Genesis 48:16: The angel who has redeemed me from all harm—may he bless these boys. And may they be called by my name and the names of my fathers Abraham and Isaac, and may they grow to be numerous within the land.

Exodus 3:2: Then the angel of the LORD appeared to him in a flame of fire within a bush. As Moses looked, he saw that the bush was on fire but was not consumed.

Exodus 14:19: Then the angel of God, who was going in front of the Israelite forces, moved and went behind them. The pillar of cloud moved from in front of them and stood behind them.

Exodus 23:20: "I am going to send an angel before you to protect you on the way and bring you to the place I have prepared."

Exodus 23:23: For my angel will go before you and bring you to the land of the Amorites, Hethites, Perizzites, Canaanites, Hivites, and Jebusites, and I will wipe them out.

Exodus 32:34: "Now go, lead the people to the place I told you about; see, my angel will go before you. But on the day I settle accounts, I will hold them accountable for their sin."

Exodus 33:2: I will send an angel ahead of you and will drive out the Canaanites, Amorites, Hethites, Perizzites, Hivites, and Jebusites.

Numbers 20:16: When we cried out to the LORD, he heard our plea, and sent an angel, and brought us out of Egypt. Now look, we are in Kadesh, a city on the border of your territory.

Numbers 22:22: But God was incensed that Balaam was going, and the angel of the LORD took his stand on the path to oppose him. Balaam was riding his donkey, and his two servants were with him.

Numbers 22:23: When the donkey saw the angel of the LORD standing on the path with a drawn sword in his hand, she turned off the path and went into the field. And Balaam hit her to return her to the path.

Numbers 22:24: Then the angel of the LORD stood in a narrow passage between the vineyards, with a stone wall on either side.

Numbers 22:25: The donkey saw the angel of the LORD and pressed herself against the wall, squeezing Balaam's foot against it. So he hit her once again.

Numbers 22:26: The angel of the LORD went ahead and stood in a narrow place where there was no room to turn to the right or the left.

Numbers 22:27: When the donkey saw the angel of the LORD, she crouched down under Balaam. So he became furious and beat the donkey with his stick.

Numbers 22:31: Then the LORD opened Balaam's eyes, and he saw the angel of the LORD standing in the path with a drawn sword in his hand. Balaam knelt low and bowed in worship on his face.

Numbers 22:32: The angel of the Lord asked him, "Why have you beaten your donkey these three times? Look, I came out to oppose you, because I consider what you are doing to be evil."

Numbers 22:34: Balaam said to the angel of the Lord, "I have sinned, for I did not know that you were standing in the path to confront me. And now, if it is evil in your sight, I will go back."

Numbers 22:35: Then the angel of the Lord said to Balaam, "Go with the men, but you are to say only what I tell you." So Balaam went on with Balak's officials.

Numbers 24:12: Balaam answered Balak, "Didn't I previously tell the messengers [angels] you sent me . . . ?"

Judges 2:1: The angel of the Lord went up from Gilgal to Bochim and said, "I brought you up out of Egypt and led you into the land I had promised to your ancestors. I also said, 'I will never break my covenant with you.'"

Judges 2:4: When the angel of the Lord had spoken these words to all the Israelites, the people wept loudly.

Judges 5:23: "Curse Meroz," says the angel of the Lord, "Bitterly curse her inhabitants, for they did not come to help the Lord, to help the Lord with the warriors."

Judges 6:11: The angel of the LORD came and sat under the oak that was in Ophrah, which belonged to Joash, the Abiezrite. His son Gideon was threshing wheat in the winepress in order to hide it from the Midianites.

Judges 6:12: Then the angel of the LORD appeared to him and said, "The LORD is with you, valiant warrior."

Judges 6:20: The angel of God said to him, "Take the meat and the unleavened bread, put it on this stone, and pour the broth on it." So he did that.

Judges 6:21: The angel of the LORD extended the tip of the staff that was in his hand and touched the meat and the unleavened bread. Fire came up from the rock and consumed the meat and the unleavened bread. Then the angel of the LORD vanished from his sight.

Judges 6:22: When Gideon realized that he was the angel of the LORD, he said, "Oh no, Lord GOD! I have seen the angel of the LORD face to face!"

Judges 6:35: And he sent messengers [angels] throughout all Manasseh, who rallied behind him. He also sent messengers throughout Asher, Zebulun, and Naphtali, who also came to meet them.

Judges 13:3: The angel of the LORD appeared to the woman and said to her, "Although you are unable to conceive and have no children, you will conceive and give birth to a son."

Judges 13:6: Then the woman went and told her husband, "A man of God came to me. He looked like the awe-inspiring angel of God. I didn't ask him where he was from, and he didn't tell me his name."

Judges 13:9: God listened to Manoah, and the angel of God came again to the woman. She was sitting in the field, and her husband, Manoah, was not with her.

Judges 13:13: The angel of the LORD answered Manoah, "Your wife needs to do everything I told her."

Judges 13:15: "Please stay here," Manoah told him [the angel of the LORD], "and we will prepare a young goat for you."

Judges 13:16: The angel of the LORD said to him, "If I stay, I won't eat your food. But if you want to prepare a burnt offering, offer it to the LORD." (Manoah did not know he was the angel of the LORD.)

Judges 13:17: Then Manoah said to him [the angel of the LORD], "What is your name, so that we may honor you when your words come true?"

Judges 13:18: "Why do you ask my name," the angel of the LORD asked him, "since it is beyond understanding?"

Judges 13:20: When the flame went up from the altar to the sky, the angel of the LORD went up in its flame. When Manoah and his wife saw this, they fell facedown on the ground.

Judges 13:21: The angel of the LORD did not appear again to Manoah and his wife. Then Manoah realized that it was the angel of the LORD.

1 Samuel 29:9: Achish answered David, "I'm convinced that you are as reliable as an angel of God. But the Philistine commanders have said, 'He must not go into battle with us.'"

2 Samuel 14:17: "Your servant thought:, May the word of my lord the king bring relief, for my lord the king is able to discern the good and the bad like the angel of God. May the LORD your God be with you."

2 Samuel 14:20: "Joab your servant has done this to address the issue indirectly, but my lord has wisdom like the wisdom of the angel of God, knowing everything on earth."

2 Samuel 19:27: Ziba slandered your servant to my lord the king. But my lord the king is like the angel of God, so do whatever you think best.

2 Samuel 24:16: Then the angel extended his hand toward Jerusalem to destroy it, but the LORD relented concerning the destruction and said to the angel who was destroying the people, "Enough, withdraw your hand now!" The angel of the Lord was then at the threshing floor of Araunah the Jebusite.

2 Samuel 24:17: When David saw the angel striking the people, he said to the Lord, "Look, I am the one who has sinned; I am the one who has done wrong. But these sheep, what have they done? Please, let your hand be against me and my father's family."

1 Kings 13:18: He said to him, "I am also a prophet like you. An angel spoke to me by the word of the Lord: 'Bring him back with you to your house so that he may eat food and drink water.'" The old prophet deceived him.

1 Kings 19:5: Then he lay down and slept under the broom tree. Suddenly, an angel touched him. The angel told him, "Get up and eat."

1 Kings 19:7: Then the angel of the Lord returned for a second time and touched him. He said, "Get up and eat, or the journey will be too much for you."

2 Kings 1:3: But the angel of the Lord said to Elijah the Tishbite, "Go and meet the messengers of the king of Samaria and say to them, 'Is it because there is no God in Israel that you are going to inquire of Baal-zebub, the god of Ekron?'"

2 Kings 1:15: The angel of the LORD said to Elijah, "Go down with him. Don't be afraid of him." So he got up and went down with him to the king.

2 Kings 19:35: That night the angel of the LORD went out and struck down one hundred eighty-five thousand in the camp of the Assyrians. When the people got up the next morning—there were all the dead bodies!

1 Chronicles 21:12: "'Three years of famine, or three months of devastation by your foes with the sword of your enemy overtaking you, or three days of the sword of the LORD—a plague on the land, the angel of the LORD bringing destruction to the whole territory of Israel.' Now decide what answer I should take back to the one who sent me."

1 Chronicles 21:15: Then God sent an angel to Jerusalem to destroy it, but as when the angel was about to destroy the city, the LORD looked, relented concerning the destruction, and said to the angel who was destroying the people, "Enough, withdraw your hand now!" The angel of the LORD was standing at the threshing floor of Ornan the Jebusite.

1 Chronicles 21:16: When David looked up and saw the angel of the LORD standing between earth and heaven, with his drawn sword in his hand stretched out over Jerusalem, David and the elders, covered in sackcloth, fell facedown.

1 Chronicles 21:18: So the angel of the LORD ordered Gad to tell David to go and set up an altar to the LORD on the threshing floor of Ornan the Jebusite.

1 Chronicles 21:20: Ornan was threshing wheat when he turned and saw the angel. His four sons, who were with him, hid.

1 Chronicles 21:27: Then the LORD spoke to the angel, and he put his sword back into its sheath.

1 Chronicles 21:30: But David could not go before it to inquire of God, because he was terrified of the sword of the LORD's angel.

2 Chronicles 32:21: And the LORD sent an angel, who annihilated every valiant warrior, leader, and commander in the camp of the king of Assyria. So the king of Assyria returned in disgrace to his land. He went to the temple of his god, and there some of his own children struck him down with the sword.

Job 4:18: If God puts no trust in his servants and he charges his angels with foolishness.

Job 33:23: If there is an angel on his side, one mediator out of the thousand, to tell a person what is right for him.

Psalm 34:7: The angel of the LORD encamps around those who fear him, and rescues them.

Psalm 35:5: Let them be like chaff in the wind, with the angel of the LORD driving them away.

Psalm 35:6: Let their way be dark and slippery, with the angel of the LORD pursuing them.

Psalm 78:49: He sent his burning anger against them: fury, indignation, and calamity—a band of deadly messengers.

Psalm 91:11: For he will give his angels orders concerning you, to protect you in all your ways.

Psalm 103:20: Bless the LORD, all his angels of great strength, who do his word, obedient to his command.

Psalm 104:4: And making the winds his messengers [angels], flames of fire his servants.

Psalm 148:2: Praise him, all his angels; praise him, all his heavenly armies.

Isaiah 37:36: Then the angel of the LORD went out and struck down one hundred eighty-five thousand in the camp of the Assyrians. When people got up the next morning, there were all the dead bodies!

Isaiah 63:9: In all their suffering, he suffered, and the angel of his presence saved them. He redeemed them because of his love and compassion; he lifted them up and carried them all the days of the past.

Hosea 12:4: Jacob struggled with the angel and prevailed; he wept and sought his favor. He found him at Bethel, and there he spoke with him.

Zechariah 1:9: I asked, "What are these, my lord?" The angel who was talking to me replied, "I will show you what they are."

Zechariah 1:11: They reported to the angel of the Lord standing among the myrtle trees, "We have patrolled the earth, and right now the whole earth is calm and quiet."

Zechariah 1:12: Then the angel of the Lord responded, "How long, Lord of Armies, will you withhold mercy from Jerusalem and the cities of Judah that you have been angry with these seventy years?"

Zechariah 1:13: The Lord replied with kind and comforting words to the angel who was speaking with me.

Zechariah 1:14: So the angel who was speaking with me said, "Proclaim: The Lord of Armies says: I am extremely jealous for Jerusalem and Zion."

Zechariah 1:19: So I asked the angel who was speaking with me, "What are these?" And he said to me, "These are the horns that scattered Judah, Israel, and Jerusalem."

Zechariah 2:3: Then the angel who was speaking with me went out, and another angel went out to meet him.

Zechariah 3:1: Then he showed me the high priest Joshua standing before the angel of the LORD, with Satan standing at his right side to accuse him.

Zechariah 3:3: Now Joshua was dressed with filthy clothes as he stood before the angel.

Zechariah 3:5: Then I said, "Let them put a clean turban on his head." So a clean turban was placed on his head, and they clothed him with garments while the angel of the LORD was standing nearby.

Zechariah 3:6: Then the angel of the LORD charged Joshua.

Zechariah 4:1: The angel who was speaking with me then returned and roused me as one awakened out of sleep.

Zechariah 4:4: Then I asked the angel who was speaking with me, "What are these, my lord?"

Zechariah 4:5: "Don't you not know what they are?" replied the angel who was speaking with me. I said, "No, my lord."

Zechariah 5:5: Then the angel who was speaking with me came forward and told me, "Look up and see what this is that is approaching."

Zechariah 5:10: So I asked the angel who was speaking with me, "Where are they taking the basket?"

Zechariah 6:4: So I inquired of the angel who was speaking with me, "What are these, my lord?"

Zechariah 6:5: The angel told me, "These are the four spirits of heaven going out after presenting themselves to the Lord of the whole earth."

Zechariah 12:8: On that day the Lord will defend the inhabitants of Jerusalem, so that on that day the one who is weakest among them will be like David on that day, and the house of David will be like God, like the angel of the Lord, before them.

Matthew 1:20: But after he had considered these things, an angel of the Lord appeared to him in a dream, saying, "Joseph, son of David, don't be afraid to take Mary as your wife, because what has been conceived in her is from the Holy Spirit."

Matthew 1:24: When Joseph woke up, he did as the Lord's angel had commanded him. He married her.

Matthew 2:13: After they were gone, an angel of the Lord appeared to Joseph in a dream, saying, "Get up! Take the child and his mother, flee to Egypt, and stay there until I tell you. For Herod is about to search for the child to kill him."

Matthew 2:19: After Herod died, an angel of the Lord appeared in a dream to Joseph in Egypt.

Matthew 4:6: And said to him, "If you are the Son of God, throw yourself down. For it is written, He will give his angels orders concerning you, and they will support you with their hands so that you will not strike your foot against a stone."

Matthew 4:11: Then the devil left him, and angels came and began to serve him.

Matthew 11:10: This is he of whom it is written, "Behold, I send my messenger before your face, who will prepare your way before you."

Matthew 13:39: And the enemy who sowed them is the devil. The harvest is the end of the age, and the harvesters are angels.

Matthew 13:41: The Son of Man will send out his angels, and they will gather from his kingdom all who causes sin and those guilty of lawlessness.

Matthew 13:49: So it will be at the end of the age. The angels will come out, separate the evil people from the righteous.

Matthew 16:27: For the Son of Man is going to come with his angels in the glory of his Father, and then he will reward each according to what he has done.

Matthew 18:10: "See to it that you don't despise one of these little ones, because I tell you that in heaven their angels continually view the face of my Father in heaven."

Matthew 22:30: For in the resurrection they neither marry nor are given in marriage but are like angels in heaven.

Matthew 24:31: He will send out his angels with a loud trumpet, and they will gather his elect from the four winds, from one end of the sky to the other.

Matthew 24:36: "Now concerning that day and hour no one knows—neither the angels of heaven nor the Son—except the Father alone."

Matthew 25:31: "When the Son of Man comes in his glory, and all the angels with him, then he will sit on his glorious throne."

Matthew 25:41: "Then he will also say to those on the left, 'Depart from me, you who are cursed, into the eternal fire prepared for the devil and his angels.'"

Matthew 26:53: Or do you think that I cannot call on my Father, and he will provide me here and now with more than twelve legions of angels?

Matthew 28:2: There was a violent earthquake, because an angel of the Lord descended from heaven and approached the tomb. He rolled back the stone and was sitting on it.

Matthew 28:5: The angel told the women, "Don't be afraid, because I know that you are looking for Jesus who was crucified."

Mark 1:2: As it is written in Isaiah the prophet, See, I am sending my messenger [angel] ahead of you; he will prepare your way.

Mark 1:13: He was in the wilderness forty days, being tempted by Satan. He was with the wild animals, and the angels were serving him.

Mark 8:38: "For whoever is ashamed of me and my words in this adulterous and sinful generation, the Son of Man will also be ashamed of him when he comes in the glory of his Father with the holy angels."

Mark 12:25: For when they rise from the dead, they neither marry nor are given in marriage but are like angels in heaven.

Mark 13:27: He will send out the angels and gather his elect from the four winds, from the ends of the earth to the ends of heaven.

Mark 13:32: "Now concerning that day or hour no one knows—neither the angels in heaven nor the Son—but only the Father."

Luke 1:11: An angel of the Lord appeared to him, standing to the right of the altar of incense.

Luke 1:13: But the angel said to him, "Do not be afraid, Zechariah, because your prayer has been heard. Your wife Elizabeth will bear you a son, and you will name him John."

Luke 1:18: "How can I know this?" Zechariah asked the angel. "For I am an old man, and my wife is well along in years."

Luke 1:19: The angel answered him, "I am Gabriel, who stands in the presence of God, and I was sent to speak to you and tell you this good news."

Luke 1:26: In the sixth month, the angel Gabriel was sent by God to a town in Galilee named Nazareth.

Luke 1:30: Then the angel told her, "Do not be afraid, Mary, for you have found favor with God."

Luke 1:34: Mary asked the angel, "How can this be, since I have not had sexual relations with a man?"

Luke 1:35: The angel replied to her, "The Holy Spirit will come upon you, and the power of the Most High will overshadow you. Therefore, the holy one to be born will be called the Son of God."

Luke 1:38: "See, I am the Lord's servant," said Mary. "May it happen to me as you have said." Then the angel left her.

Luke 2:9: Then an angel of the Lord stood before them, and the glory of the Lord shone around them, and they were terrified.

Luke 2:10: But the angel said to them, "Don't be afraid, for look, I proclaim to you good news of great joy that will be for all the people."

Luke 2:13: Suddenly there was a multitude of the heavenly host with the angel, praising God and saying, . . .

Luke 2:15: When the angels had left them and returned to heaven, the shepherds said to one another, "Let's go straight to Bethlehem and see what has happened, which the Lord has made known to us."

Luke 2:21: When the eight days were completed for his circumcision, he was named Jesus—the name given by the angel before he was conceived.

Luke 4:10: For it is written, He will give his angels orders concerning you, to protect you.

Luke 7:24: After John's messengers left, he began to speak to the crowds about John: "What did you go out into the wilderness to see? A reed shaken by the wind?"

Luke 7:27: This is the one about whom it is written, See, I am sending my messenger [angel] ahead of you; he will prepare your way before you.

Luke 9:26: For whoever is ashamed of me and of my words, the Son of Man will be ashamed of him when he comes in his glory and that of the Father and the holy angels.

Luke 9:52: He sent messengers ahead of himself, and on the way they entered a village of the Samaritans to make preparations for him.

Luke 12:8: "And I say to you, anyone who acknowledges me before others, the Son of Man will also acknowledge before the angels of God."

Luke 12:9: But whoever denies me before others will be denied before the angels of God.

Luke 15:10: "I tell you, in the same way, there is joy in the presence of God's angels over one sinner who repents."

Luke 16:22: One day the poor man died and was carried by the angels to Abraham's side. The rich man also died and was buried.

Luke 22:43: Then an angel from heaven appeared to him, strengthening him.

Luke 24:23: And when they didn't find his body, they came and reported that they had seen a vision of angels who said he was alive.

John 1:51: Then he said, "Truly I tell you, you will see heaven opened and the angels of God ascending and descending on the Son of Man."

John 12:29: The crowd standing there heard it and said it was thunder. Others said, "An angel has spoken to him."

John 20:12: She saw two angels in white sitting where Jesus's body had been lying, one at the head and the other at the feet.

Acts 5:19: But an angel of the Lord opened the doors of the jail during the night, brought them out, and said, . . .

Acts 6:15: And all who were sitting in the Sanhedrin looked intently at him and saw that his face was like the face of an angel.

Acts 7:30: After forty years had passed, an angel appeared to him in the wilderness of Mount Sinai, in a flame of fire in a bush.

Acts 7:35: "This Moses, whom they rejected when they said, Who appointed you a ruler and a judge?—this one God sent as a ruler and a deliverer through the angel who appeared to him in the bush."

Acts 7:38: He is the one who was in the assembly in the wilderness, with the angel who spoke to him at Mount Sinai, and with our ancestors. He received living oracles to give to us.

Acts 7:53: You received the law under the direction of angels and yet have not kept it.

Acts 8:26: An angel of the Lord spoke to Philip: "Get up and go south to the road that goes down from Jerusalem to Gaza." (This is the desert road.)

Acts 10:3: About three in the afternoon he distinctly saw in a vision an angel of God who came in and said to him, "Cornelius."

Acts 10:7: When the angel who spoke to him had gone, he called two of his household servants and a devout soldier, who was one of those who attended him.

Acts 10:22: They said, "Cornelius, a centurion, an upright and God-fearing man, who has a good reputation with the whole Jewish nation, was divinely directed by a holy angel to call you to his house and to hear a message from you."

Acts 11:13: He reported to us how he had seen the angel standing in his house and saying, "Send to Joppa, and call for Simon, who is also named Peter."

Acts 12:7: Suddenly an angel of the Lord appeared, and a light shone in the cell. Striking Peter on the side, he woke him up and said, "Quick, get up!" And the chains fell off his wrists.

Acts 12:8: "Get dressed," the angel told him, and put on your sandals." And he did. "Wrap your cloak around you," he told him, "and follow me."

Acts 12:9: So he went out and followed, and he did not know that what the angel did was really happening, but he thought he was seeing a vision.

Acts 12:10: After they passed the first and second guards, they came to the iron gate that leads into the city, which opened to them by itself. They went outside and passed one street, and suddenly the angel left him.

Acts 12:11: When Peter came to himself, he said, "Now I know for certain that the Lord has sent his angel and rescued me from Herod's grasp and from all that the Jewish people expected."

Acts 12:15: "You're out of your mind!" they told her. But she kept insisting that it was true, and they said, "It's his angel."

Acts 12:23: At once an angel of the Lord struck him because he did not give the glory to God, and he was eaten by worms and died.

Acts 23:8: For the Sadducees say there is no resurrection, and neither angel nor spirit, but the Pharisees affirm them all.

Acts 23:9: The shouting grew loud, and some of the scribes of the Pharisees' party got up and argued vehemently, "We find nothing evil in this man. What if a spirit or an angel has spoken to him?"

Acts 27:23: For last night an angel of the God I belong to and serve stood by me.

Romans 8:38: For I am persuaded that neither death nor life, nor angels nor rulers, nor things present nor things to come, nor powers.

1 Corinthians 4:9: For I think that God has displayed us, the apostles, in last place, like men condemned to die: We have become a spectacle to the world, both to angels and to people.

1 Corinthians 6:3: Don't you know that we will judge angels—how much more matters of this life!

1 Corinthians 11:10: This is why a woman should have a symbol of authority on her head, because of the angels.

1 Corinthians 13:1: If I speak human or angelic tongues but do not have love, I am a noisy gong or a clanging cymbal.

2 Corinthians 11:14: And no wonder! For Satan disguises himself as an angel of light.

2 Corinthians 12:7: Especially because of the extraordinary revelations. Therefore, so that I would not exalt myself, a thorn in the flesh was given to me, a messenger [angel] of Satan to torment me so that I would not exalt myself.

Galatians 1:8: But even if we or an angel from heaven should preach to you a gospel contrary to what we have preached to you, a curse be on him!

Galatians 3:19: Why, then, was the law given? It was added for the sake of transgressions until the Seed to whom the promise was made would come. The law was put into effect through angels by means of a mediator.

Galatians 4:14: You did not despise or reject me though my physical condition was a trial for you. On the contrary, you received me as an angel of God, as Christ Jesus himself.

Colossians 2:18: Let no one condemn you by delighting in ascetic practices and the worship of angels, claiming access to a visionary realm. Such people are inflated by his empty notions of their unspiritual mind.

2 Thessalonians 1:7: And to give relief to you who are afflicted, along with us. This will take place at the revelation of the Lord Jesus from heaven with his powerful angels.

1 Timothy 3:16: And most certainly, the mystery of godliness is great: He was manifested in the flesh, vindicated in the Spirit, seen by angels, preached among the nations, believed on in the world, taken up in glory.

1 Timothy 5:21: I solemnly charge you before God and Christ Jesus and the elect angels to observe these things without prejudice, doing nothing out of favoritism.

Hebrews 1:4: So he became superior to the angels, just as the name he inherited is more excellent than theirs.

Hebrews 1:5: For to which of the angels did he ever say, You are my Son; today I have become your Father, or again, I will be his Father, and he will be my Son?

Hebrews 1:6: Again, when he brings the firstborn into the world, he says, "And let all God's angels worship him."

Hebrews 1:7: And about the angels he says, He makes his angels winds, and his servants a fiery flame.

Hebrews 1:13: Now to which of the angels has he ever said, Sit at my right hand until I make your enemies your footstool?

Hebrews 2:2: For if the message spoken through angels was legally binding and every transgression and disobedience received a just punishment.

Hebrews 2:5: For he has not subjected to angels the world to come that we are talking about.

Hebrews 2:7: You made him lower than the angels for a short time; you crowned him with glory and honor.

Hebrews 2:9: But we do see Jesus—made lower than the angels for a short time so that by God's grace he might taste death for everyone—crowned with glory and honor because he suffered death.

Hebrews 2:16: For it is clear that he does not reach out to help angels, but to help Abraham's offspring.

Hebrews 12:22: Indeed, you have come to Mount Zion, to the city of the living God (the heavenly Jerusalem), to myriads of angels, a festive gathering.

Hebrews 13:2: Don't neglect to show hospitality, for by doing this some have welcomed angels as guests without knowing it.

1 Peter 1:12: It was revealed to them that they were not serving themselves but you. These things have now been announced to you through those who preached the gospel to you by the Holy Spirit sent from heaven—angels long to catch a glimpse of these things.

1 Peter 3:22: Who has gone into heaven and is at the right hand of God with angels, authorities, and powers subject to him.

2 Peter 2:4: For if God didn't spare the angels who sinned but cast them into hell and delivered them in chains of utter darkness to be kept for judgment.

2 Peter 2:11: However, angels, who are greater in might and power, do not bring a slanderous charge against them before the Lord.

Jude 6: And the angels who did not keep their own position but abandoned their proper dwelling, he has kept in eternal chains for the judgment on the great day.

Revelation 1:1: The revelation of Jesus Christ that God gave him to show his servants what must soon take place. He made it known by sending his angel to his servant John.

Revelation 3:5: "In the same way, the one who conquers will be dressed in white clothes, and I will never erase his name from the book of life but will acknowledge his name before my Father and before his angels."

Revelation 5:2: I also saw a mighty angel proclaiming with a loud voice, "Who is worthy to open the scroll and break its seals?"

Revelation 5:11: Then I looked and heard the voice of many angels around the throne, and also of the living creatures and of the elders. Their number was countless thousands, plus thousands of thousands.

Revelation 7:1: After this I saw four angels standing at the four corners of the earth, restraining the four winds of the earth so that no wind could blow on the earth or the sea or on any tree.

Revelation 7:2: Then I saw another angel rising up from the east, who had the seal of the living God. He cried out in a loud voice to the four angels who were allowed to harm the earth and the sea.

Revelation 7:11: All the angels stood around the throne, and along with the elders and the four living creatures they fell facedown before the throne and worshiped God.

Revelation 8:2: Then I saw the seven angels who stand in the presence of God; seven trumpets were given to them.

Revelation 8:3: Another angel, with a golden incense burner, came and stood at the altar. He was given a large amount of incense to offer with the prayers of all the saints on the golden altar in front of the throne.

Revelation 8:4: The smoke of the incense, with the prayers of the saints, went up in the presence of God from the angel's hand.

Revelation 8:5: The angel took the incense burner, filled it with fire from the altar, and hurled it to the earth; there were peals of thunder, rumblings, flashes of lightning, and an earthquake.

Revelation 8:6: And the seven angels who had the seven trumpets prepared to blow them.

Revelation 8:7: The first angel blew his trumpet, and hail and fire, mixed with blood, were hurled to the earth. So a third of the earth was burned up, a third of the trees were burned up, and all the green grass was burned up.

Revelation 8:8: The second angel blew his trumpet, and something like a great mountain ablaze with fire was hurled into the sea. So a third of the sea became blood.

Revelation 8:10: The third angel blew his trumpet, and a great star, blazing like a torch, fell from heaven. It fell on a third of the rivers and on the springs of water.

Revelation 8:12: The fourth angel blew his trumpet, and a third of the sun was struck, a third of the moon, and a third of the stars, so that a third of them were darkened. A third of the day was without light and also a third of the night.

Revelation 8:13: I looked and heard an eagle flying high overhead, crying out in a loud voice, "Woe! Woe! Woe to those who live on the earth, because of the remaining trumpet blasts that the three angels are about to sound!"

Revelation 9:1: The fifth angel blew his trumpet, and I saw a star that had fallen from heaven to earth. The key for the shaft to the abyss was given to him.

Revelation 9:11: They had as king the angel of the abyss; his name in Hebrew is Abaddon, and in Greek he has the name Apollyon.

Revelation 9:13: The sixth angel blew his trumpet. From the four horns of the golden altar that is before God, I heard a voice.

Revelation 9:14: Say to the sixth angel who had the trumpet, "Release the four angels bound at the great river Euphrates."

Revelation 9:15: So the four angels who were prepared for the hour, day, month, and year were released to kill a third of the human race.

Revelation 10:1: Then I saw another mighty angel coming down from heaven, wrapped in a cloud, with a rainbow over his head. His face was like the sun, his legs were like pillars of fire.

Revelation 10:5: Then the angel that I had seen standing on the sea and on the land raised his right hand to heaven.

Revelation 10:7: "But in the days when the seventh angel will blow his trumpet, then the mystery of God will be completed, as he announced to his servants the prophets."

Revelation 10:8: Then the voice that I had heard from heaven spoke to me again and said, "Go, take the scroll that lies open in the hand of the angel who is standing on the sea and on the land."

Revelation 10:9: So I went to the angel and asked him to give me the little scroll. He said to me, "Take and eat it; it will be bitter in your stomach, but it will be as sweet as honey in your mouth."

Revelation 10:10: Then I took the little scroll from the angel's hand and ate it. It was as sweet as honey in my mouth, but when I ate it my stomach became bitter.

Revelation 11:15: The seventh angel blew his trumpet, and there were loud voices in heaven saying, The kingdom of the world has become the kingdom of our Lord and of his Christ, and he will reign forever and ever.

Revelation 12:7: Then war broke out in heaven: Michael and his angels fought against the dragon. The dragon and his angels fought.

Revelation 12:9: So the great dragon was thrown out—the ancient serpent, who is called the devil and Satan, the one who deceives the whole world. He was thrown to the earth, and his angels with him.

Revelation 14:6: Then I saw another angel flying high overhead, with the eternal gospel to announce to the inhabitants of the earth—to every nation, tribe, language, and people.

Revelation 14:8: And another, a second angel, followed, saying, "It has fallen, Babylon the great has fallen. She made all the nations drink the wine of her sexual immorality, which brings wrath."

Revelation 14:9: And another, a third angel, followed them and spoke with a loud voice: "If anyone worships the beast and its image and receives a mark on his forehead or on his hand, . . ."

Revelation 14:10: ". . . he will also drink the wine of God's wrath, which is poured full strength into the cup of his anger. He will be tormented with fire and sulfur in the sight of the holy angels and in the sight of the Lamb."

Revelation 14:15: Another angel came out of the temple, crying out with a loud voice to the one who was seated on the cloud, "Use your sickle and reap, for the time to reap has come, since the harvest of the earth is ripe."

Revelation 14:17: Then another angel who also had a sharp sickle came out of the temple in heaven.

Revelation 14:18: Yet another angel, who had authority over the fire, came from the altar, and he called with a loud voice to the one who had the sharp sickle, "Use your sharp sickle and gather the clusters of grapes from the vineyard of the earth, because its grapes have ripened."

Revelation 14:19: So the angel swung his sickle across the earth and gathered the grapes from the vineyard of the earth, and he threw them into the great winepress of God's wrath.

Revelation 15:1: Then I saw another great and awe-inspiring sign in heaven: seven angels with the seven last plagues; for with them God's wrath will be completed.

Revelation 15:6: Out of the temple came the seven angels with the seven plagues, dressed in pure, bright linen, with golden sashes wrapped around their chests.

Revelation 15:7: One of the four living creatures gave the seven angels seven golden bowls filled with the wrath of God who lives forever and ever.

Revelation 15:8: Then the temple was filled with smoke from the glory of God and from his power, and no one could enter the temple until the seven plagues of the seven angels were completed.

Revelation 16:1: Then I heard a loud voice from the temple saying to the seven angels, "Go and pour out the seven bowls of God's wrath on the earth."

Revelation 16:5: I heard the angel of the waters say, "You are just, the Holy One, who is and who was, because you have passed judgment on these things."

Revelation 17:1: Then one of the seven angels who had the seven bowls came and spoke with me: "Come, I will show you the judgment of the notorious prostitute who is seated on many waters."

Revelation 17:7: Then the angel said to me, "Why are you astonished? I will explain to you the mystery of the woman and of the beast, with the seven heads and the ten horns, that carries her."

Revelation 18:1: After this I saw another angel with great authority coming down from heaven, and the earth was illuminated by his splendor.

Revelation 18:21: Then a mighty angel picked up a stone like a large millstone and threw it into the sea, saying, In this way, Babylon the great city will be thrown down violently and never be found again.

Revelation 19:17: Then I saw an angel standing in the sun, and he called out in a loud voice, saying to all the birds flying overhead, "Come, gather together for the great supper of God."

Revelation 20:1: Then I saw an angel coming down from heaven holding in his hand the key to the abyss and a great chain in his hand.

Revelation 21:9: Then one of the seven angels, who had held the seven bowls filled with the seven last plagues, came and spoke to me: "Come, I will show you the bride, the wife of the Lamb."

Revelation 21:12: The city had a massive high wall, with twelve gates. Twelve angels were at the gates; the names of the twelve tribes of Israel's sons were inscribed on the gates.

Revelation 21:17: Then he measured its wall, 144 cubits to human measurement, which the angel used.

Revelation 22:6: Then he said to me, "These words are faithful and true. The Lord, the God of the spirits of the prophets, has sent his angel to show his servants what must soon take place."

Revelation 22:8: I, John, am the one who heard and saw these things. When I heard and saw them, I fell down to worship at the feet of the angel who had shown them to me.

Revelation 22:16: "I, Jesus, have sent my angel to attest these things to you for the churches. I am the Root and the descendant of David, the bright morning star."

About the Author

John R. Gilhooly is a professor of philosophy and theology who helps students and church members think Christianly and critically about their faith and their world. He is director of the Honors Program at Cedarville University in Cedarville, Ohio, where he teaches classes on logic, the history of philosophy, angelology, and humanity.

John has written or edited several books, including *Philosophy of Religion and Art, Evil—and a Selection of Its Theological Problems* and *The Devil's Own Luck*. His academic publications have appeared in *Philosophia Christi, The Journal for Septuagint and Cognate Studies,* and *The International Journal of Philosophy, Science, and Religion.*

Dr. Gilhooly lives in southwest Ohio with his wife, Ginger, a professor of writing, and his three children, Caleb (connoisseur of maps and flags), Carson (slayer of dragons), and Ellie (master of horses and unicorns).